# RECUERDOS

**Written by Robert Avila**

FlowerSong Press



ISBN: 978-1-953447-18-0

Published by FlowerSong Press in the United States of America.

www.flowersongpress.com

Cover Design by SageLight Design

Set in Adobe Garamond Pro



NOTICE: SCHOOLS AND BUSINESSES

FlowerSong Press offers copies of this book at a quantity discount with bulk purchases for educational, business, or sales promotional use. For information, please email the Publisher at info@flowersong-press.com.

# CHAPTER ONE

I can remember the day that it happened almost as though it was yesterday. If you were to get all of the parties involved, me, my brother Rick, my sister Ida and my mother and my grandmother, each one of them would have a different account of the story. I may not remember the exact timeline of how it happened, but I do know that I remember EXACTLY what transpired since it happened to me.

I am standing in the main ballroom of the beautiful Empire Club. Today is my last official day before I enter the world of retirement from my 20-year career as a federal agent. I have climbed up the ladder, retiring at the highest rank. It has been quite a journey. There are people that I have enjoyed and those who enjoyed me, those that I have endured and those whom I have influenced. It has been a long ride. I greet the many people who stop by to wish me well as they send me out into the unknown world of retirement. I have become somewhat reminiscent of waiting for the ceremony to start. The table on the dais is full of well-wishers and pranksters dutifully bound to send me off into my next phase of life, with as much humor and embarrassment as they can muster at my expense. I stand off to the side of the room in my gray pinstripe suit wondering whether this moment is real. I had often imagined this phase in my life. Now that it is finally here it seems surreal.

My mind wanders as I wait for the invited guests to stop by for a hug or a handshake. I am pondering over the question just posed to me by my old partner Victor who felt it his duty to bring over two shots of tequila for a goodbye toast. Funny, when he first came up to me I thought they were both for him.

"Hey, you made it and not too worse for wear huh," he says as he reluctantly hands me the shot glass.

"Yeah, and now that it's here, it doesn't seem as long as all that." I say thinking to myself, isn't that the way it always is? You go through something in life anticipating its ultimate finale by dreaming of the day it will be over. When it is, you wonder where all the time went. "There is no way twenty years have slipped by." I inform my old friend and partner.

"Salud, dinero y amor," Victor says as he downs the shot in one swift motion. "So tell me man-of-the-hour, if you could name one particular person that you can say really influenced your life. One person who helped you stand here today, who would that person be?"

I look at him. As I start to digest the question posed, other friends and coworkers stop by with tidings of goodbye and good luck. By the time I finish with this group, other friends stop by. Victor wanders back to the table where his wife Bonnie is sitting without a reply. I really had intended to provide an answer to his question. I felt like talking but I could see her at their table, pointing her finger warning him about those tequila shots. Telling him how emotional he got when he had more than three. I move over to my designated spot behind the curtain where I had been told to stand while I wait for the folks at the head table to start their introductory remarks. My mind drifts off into my own thoughts.

Victor's question was one for which I had known the answer to at a very young age. One that took me to the very beginning. One that caused me to remember someone that had been gone for a long time. Way back to the day, when the person with the single most influence on me first came into my life, or as best as my memory can go back. Given that she had been around since the day when I first came into this world. Grandma Lencha was at best unique and at worst well, no one really called her anything when she was at her worst. No one had ever dared to. Even the way she looked at things was slanted in her favor, though she could be the cause of the problem. Nobody ever had the guts to confront her as being the cause. My guess is that because of that she never thought she was at fault. My emotional attachment to her first started when I was a small child. Which brings me back to the story etched so well in my memory.

Growing up in the border town of El Paso teaches you two things to help you survive this life. You learn to be tough and you learn to live on laughter. You find out very early that life can be a cruel journey. Money is a rare commodity in the barrios of the Southside of El Paso. The hard lessons I experienced without it made me appreciate today all the more. In order to appreciate this success, I first had to attend the school of hard knocks where my grandmother had tenure as an instructor.

In life, you must have a mentor to avoid the pitfalls that doom you to a life wasted on the streets. Someone who's been there and yet managed to overcome its pitfalls. The student must appreciate and respect the mentor, and in turn, the mentor must show true care for the student. This was my relationship with my grandmother. I despised the lessons where she pushed me to the extreme for I thought she was doing so to punish me. Today I stand here, appreciative of the fact I was lucky and wise enough to have survived to tell about it. She taught me an understanding of life's lessons. The end justifies the means. As a young child, I didn't understand this. I recall having this strong dislike for those times when I didn't understand her methods of punishment, as was evident by the story.

On this particular occasion, my brother and I were running around my grandma Lencha's house while my mother was at work. My grandmother would baby-sit while my older sisters were expected to help with the chores. I was eleven and my brother was nine. We didn't have anything productive to do except cause havoc in the house. It was a small place. Years later, I went back to see it when they were getting ready to tear it down, it seemed even smaller.

We were playing a mean game of hide and go seek. My brother came around the corner into the kitchen and ran right into my grandma Lencha who was busy preparing lunch for my grandfather. She was making *arroz con nopales y huevo*. Even in my recollections of those times, my mouth still waters from the smell. I could swear, for a moment, the curtains here at the Empire Club had the same aroma of her kitchen. Anyway, when my brother came around the corner and crashed into her faded white apron he almost spilled the *arroz* on the floor. She had a typical Mexican grandmotherly response to this mocoso child running around the sacred workplace known as her kitchen.

*"Chavalo shingado, que no ves que ya mero me haces que tire este arroz. Lárguen-se para fuera y ponganse de pie a hacer algo. Y no salgan a la calle cabrones o les doy un jalon de mechas."* Roughly translated, my grandmother was a bit irritated by the near spill. She politely asked if we would be so kind as to go play outside. Anywhere outside as long as it was out of her sight. Oh and by the way, please be so kind as to not to play in the street because if you did, you would be dead. Your death would not come by way of a car hitting you but would be the result of her murdering you for playing there.

This was the general thought on her mind. At the age of eleven, I did not know any better. I thought all grandmothers talked like this. This was just her way of showing how much she loved us. I recall other times when she was drinking and would talk to us in a similar fashion. Her favorite drink was rum and coke. I thought all grandmothers drank rum and coke.

As a child, I would run into the garage and grab a coke from the boxes of sodas we had brought from Juarez the Sunday before at the Mercado. In those days, it cost three dollars for a box of sodas. My grandfather would stack them up outside in the garage. It wasn't so much a garage as it was a carport covered with chicken wire and *laminas* that passed for a roof. If chickens ever attacked the family car, I figured it would be safe since it was surrounded with so much wire.

The back wall was made up of aluminum siding that my Tio Manuel had brought home from the Sears department store where he worked. He would tell my grandmother that the gringos had ordered too much of it and that el Sr. Leonir (Leonard) had told him it was OK to take some home. It was commonplace for my uncle who worked at Sears to bring home new things in sealed boxes that he said Mr. Leonir had told him it was OK to take.

After I brought her the bottle of coke, she would then tell me to bring the bottle on top of the refrigerator. I didn't know what alcohol was, I only knew she wanted me to bring her a bottle with the letters R-U-M on it.

"*Andale cabron, y traime la botella de Bacardi y no la tires porque ahorita te doy un jalón de greñas*…" my grandmother would add gingerly.

After drinking two or three of these, she would always call me over and give me a quarter or tell me what a good boy I was. This, of course, was while she hugged and kissed me on the cheek pinching it till it turned red.

Her usual response was, "*Hay tan bueno y tan lindo mi cabroncito, mira nomas pero Dios mio.*"

I could smell the liquor on her breath along with a strong odor of tobacco. She had an ashtray close by with her PALL MALLS, the unfiltered ones they sold back then. There was always one lit next in the ashtray next to her or in her hand. I was used to seeing her be a sweet and caring person.

But I had also seen her be a mean spirited woman who did not think twice about back slapping you if you pissed her off.

My grandma Lencha was always saying *cabron* or *pinche* to us. I didn't think anything of it when we were told to go out and play. Not even when she said she would kill us if she caught us playing in the street. I thought all grandmothers were like that. So on this particular day, we went outside looking for a place to continue our juvenile plundering. My grandma's house was on Radford Street. We lived on the first block of a six block long street where train tracks separated the first and the second block and beyond. Anytime we were eating at the table and the trains rolled by on the tracks, the little house would shake. We learned to pick up our bottle of soda or glass and hold it in our hands since the little table in the little kitchen would rattle so much. Of course grandma Lencha would pick up her rum and coke and always say the same thing, "*aahh ese pinche tren como cay mal.*" The train would go by and we would all go back to whatever we were eating. But even the train location didn't compare to the biggest adventure found when exploring my grandma's house. The biggest thing we found fascinating about staying over there was that right behind the swing set my tio Manuel had brought home one day (of course from Sears), was what lay on the opposite side of the chain link fence. Right behind the fence that separated the properties was the Evergreen cemetery, one of the oldest cemeteries in the city. If you stood at my grandma Lencha's kitchen and looked through the little window on the door you could see the tombstones with the granite markers and the crosses strategically placed throughout the cemetery.

Apparently when the city had first built the cemetery, they kept expanding it little by little in order to meet the growing demands of the trade. Now, all these years later, the backyard of the little houses on Radford Street butted up to the new sections of the cemetery. All the houses on the street had a view of the cemetery from their back doors.

On this particular day when my grandmother had issued orders to get out of the house, my brother Rick and I found a spot in the backyard next to the swings along the fence line. There my grandfather had dumped piles of dirt for mixing with cement. For years he had planned on laying concrete in the back yard where the adults could gather to drink and dance. At least this had been the plan two years ago and although he kept saying it, he never really got around to doing it. Still, it made a great play area and all my cousins and me and my brother would get together and wrestle in the dirt, play war games and generally just allow our imaginations to take over.

# CHAPTER TWO

Banished to the outdoors by our grandmother, my brother and I dad decided to play war games. Now war games played in the barrios are different from Anglo war games. In the Anglo version, you have toy soldiers that your parents buy down at the Walgreens or at the old Toys by Roy stores in town. When I got a little older, I even lifted some. Oops I mean I had SEEN some at the store with a matching tank and jeep. Man those were nice. You could place the plastic toys on the hills and pretend enemy bombardments were attacking your soldiers. Counterattacks were executed and war waged on as fiercely as only a child's imagination can invent.

In Chicano war games, you didn't have toy soldiers. You collect those old Popsicle sticks people throw away after they eat the ice cream off it. You collected as many as you could. Then you glue them together and create the impression of a small wall fort that protects your soldiers from the advancing army. The soldiers are made up of matches stolen from your father's matchbox. The generals of the army were shiny nails. Other officer figures came from the variety of bolts and screws you would find in the street and save in order to play soldiers. If you found a bolt and screw set intact, then the bolt was considered a captain and the screw was a tank. Of course, you had to call what everything was before you could start any game. Any nails not identified as soldiers were considered against the rules of the game. You were then made fun of by your adversary by being called a *tapado*, which roughly translated meant idiot.

Of course, no one realized the absurdity of the whole matter or understood that we were truly all *tapados*. But necessity is the mother of invention and we made do with what we had. Attack formations were not always restricted to advancing your forces as a group. In Chicano war games, rocks took the place of incoming missiles. In this scenario, you would heave a rock at your opponent's soldiers and try to inflict as much damage as possible. The side with the most casualties would lose the war and at that point, you would start another war with different rules of engagement.

Trouble is that in the attempt to kill your opponent's army, the more casualties you could inflict in one sweep the better your chances were for survival. It stands to reason that the bigger the rock, the more damage to your opponent. Anything was allowed as long as it was made of rock, stone or metal and as long as it could be thrown from one encampment to another (Don't ask me why, I don't make up these rules). As the battle raged, my brother and I busily bombed each other's embankment. I spotted a large rock covered by dirt that had hardened from the rains of the previous week and figured it would no doubt cause considerable damage upon impact. The dirt caked on it would explode on impact causing a wide area of damage.

I picked up the rock, and as per the rules, each side was allowed to get a good bead on the enemy's placement thus making an air strike more viable. I could see the enemy soldiers on the small hill in front of my brother who was pinned down behind his soldier battalion made up of matches, sticks and assorted other household items serving as his transportation and supply groups. I particularly liked the can of beer that passed as a lookout station with a little nail on top as the forward outpost. I thought that was a nice touch.

In his mind, my brother thought he was GI Joe huddled down behind his troops ready to give orders at a moment's notice. He was embedded behind the hill lying on his stomach to the side of his troops waiting his turn to return the newfound explosion device I now held in my hand.

I studied his troop placement and made ready to throw the rock as high in the air as I possibly could to cause as much damage as possible. As I heaved the rock into the air, I let out a whizzing sound that made it sound as though enemy planes were dropping their two- ton payload on the enemy forces. The only thing was that my aim had been just a bit off. In my attempt at mastering the ability to hit the center of the mass of soldiers and cause as much chaos to the enemy forces as possible, I had leaned over to the left giving it a little too much uummpphh! I looked up at the rock as it reached its highest apex and started its downward spiral. I looked directly down at the anticipated point of impact. In doing so, I noticed that the general area would not be where I had initially aimed. Instead it was a direct impact hit for the area currently occupied by my little brother.

There are times in life when you can see something terrible about to happen but are powerless to do anything about it. As in anticipating a car wreck, or when you see someone riding a bike and they aren't looking at where they're going, and so on. You generally just stare at the point of impact and wait for the inevitable with a pained look on your face. Running to try and get them out of the way will just not do it. So all you can do is crunch your face and stand in an awkward pose waiting for the inevitable.

My brother looked up to locate the rock hurled into the air. As I saw this, the only thing I could think was that I hoped he had enough sense to close his eyes to minimize the damage, or turn away. Anything, as long as the damage would be kept to a minimum. The fact that I was in trouble was already a given. I was going to pay for this and pay for it big time. My hope, at this point, was that maybe my *tapado* brother would have enough sense to see the object in the sky and attempt to move out of the way. He didn't. He looked straight at the rock. Luckily, he looked down right before it hit him in the back of the head causing him to shove his face into the dirt.

The back of his head swelled and at first I thought he was out cold. But when I heard him start to cry and reach back to hold his head I ran over to him. My thoughts started racing. Immediately I took inventory of all my worldly possessions to see if there was anything of value to entice my brother into keeping quiet on my part in this matter. Realizing I had nothing, I ran over to see if he was OK. My grandmother was going to be really pissed off. In about an hour, I was going to be dead, buried in one of those empty holes in the cemetery on the other side of the fence. My grandmother would make sure of that.

My brother was stumbling around trying to get on his feet, crying. I knew he was going to head for the house to tell on me. My mind worked fast and furious trying to think of something to say to prevent my date with the executioner, grandma Lencha.

"*Hey pendejo*, I told you to duck." This was not true, I had only yelled out the required whoosh sound of the plane doors opening to drop their bombs. My brother got up and pointed himself in the direction of the house.

"Hey, remember that red Tonka truck you saw at Western Auto the other day? Say you slipped and landed on your face and hit yourself on a rock and I'll steal it for you. You'd like that, huh?" I knew I could not make good on this promise. I had been banned from the Western Auto store when caught trying to steal a bag of those soft rubber balls that I had planned on using for future war games. Man, I wish I had not gotten caught. With those balls in hand, I would not be in this predicament and *shingado*!

My brother was crying louder now and walking towards the back door of the house calling for grandma Lencha. The knot on his head had grown in size too. The back of his head, I thought, looked like one of those Martians that you used to see on TV. The ones that arrive in a spaceship, walking out with two heads on a little body ready to take over the earth. AAAHHHH!

I laughed only for a moment as the dread of the pending beating from my grandma Lencha came back into my thoughts. I shuddered with fear. There was no way he was going to stop. Boy I was going to really get it now.

I tried one last tactic, hoping that, although sacrilegious in nature, I hoped it would do the trick and prevent him from reporting me to the authorities.

"Hey, you better not say it was my fault because grandma Lencha is gonna take me to the tracks and tie me up and the next train that comes by is gonna run over me and you're not gonna have a brother anymore!" This was also not true. My grandma Lencha, as mean as she could be, would never tie a little boy up on any train tracks. Besides, it didn't seem to faze him as he kept crying and walking towards the house.

As he opened the screen door and went into the kitchen, my mind raced at a million miles trying to figure out what the punishment would be. I seriously thought about running off and not coming back, ever, NEVER! I was only eleven, yet I knew the chances of surviving out in the world with no job and no money were slim to none. Hell, it was a struggle to survive here in this neighborhood much less someplace else. I could hear the wailing coming from inside the house. I could also hear the questions being posed by my grandma Lencha who was now screaming at him, trying to find out what happened.

She freaked out at seeing my brother looking like a two headed monster. She wanted to know what had caused him to look so deformed, much more than usual as far as I was concerned.

My older sister Ida stood ahead of me in the family chain. She was three years older than I was. She enjoyed running track at school and was damn good at it. She had these long legs that made her one of the better track stars at the middle school she attended. I heard my grandmother call out to her from inside the house. I knew that at this point my sister Ida would be the enforcer for my grandma Lencha.

You see, my grandma didn't believe that she should expel any more force than necessary to get anything done. She felt that as head matriarch of the family, she was entitled to issue orders expecting those entrusted under her to carry them out without asking questions. This was a smart theory on her part since we were ALL scared of my grandma Lencha.

As I said, when grandma wanted to she could be one of the nicest and sweetest person on this earth. She would love you by hugging you tight and smothering you with kisses, telling you that you were just the perfect child. But when she was in a bad mood, holy s*#%! She had a way of looking at you that put the fear of God into the bottom of your soul.

She was a petite woman who had survived two husbands. She was married to a third whom she kept on a short leash. Her father, a Mexican married to a Spanish woman, had survived the brutal Mexican revolution years of the early 1900's. One of twenty-one children born to my great-grandparents, my grandmother had learned the struggles of life early on. Her father had been a young man in his teens when he stowed away on a boat bound for Spain at the turn of the century.

In Spain, he had joined a traveling circus. There he met my great grandmother who was a seamstress for the circus. Together they traveled around the country. My great grandfather worked as a circus hand until someone asked if he wanted to learn how to be a trapeze performer. He had a tall lanky body and good upper strength. The circus owners felt he was ideal for the job. So he agreed, learning the trade so well in fact, that he was able to put money away for himself and his new bride. The circus then toured the bigger cities in Mexico and it was after that tour that he decided to take his money and buy a mercantile store in Chihuahua Mexico.

In the early part of this century, with civil war looming in Mexico, times were very uncertain. My grandmother would tell me countless tales of her family's struggle. Her mother, my great grandmother, was not so sure that buying a store was a good idea. My great grandfather reassured her that what he was doing was the right thing. So they bought a supply store that stocked grain, feed and other general store items.

When civil war broke out, the revolutionary leader Pancho Villa started making runs to the border town of Ciudad Juarez to trade for weapons and guns from the gringos in the United States. On the way there, Villa would often stop off at my great grandfather's store to purchase supplies.

I had a great fascination for my grandmother's stories. I imagined her as a young child through those perilous times. To think that she had actually been through these events and lived to tell me was better than going to any library. The great storyteller would make history come to life and I always listened intently to stories about the early days of her childhood.

Apparently when the war first started, things were going bad for Villa and his men. My grandmother would tell me that his pounding at the door would awaken her mother and father in the middle of the night. They lived in the back of the store with their children. The family would be rousted from their sleep and ordered by Villa to fix something to eat. Since he was a bandit on the run from the federal authorities with very little money, Villa would take what he needed as provisions for his men. My grandmother's mother said that when he had money, he would pay for what he took. More often than not though he wouldn't. He was saving his money to buy guns and ammunition from the gringos in El Paso. Revolutions, after all, can be very expensive.

The civil war turned the country into a nightmare. My great-grand-father's dream of living in peace tending to his beloved store was fading because of the war so he decided to move his family to the United States. They had endured humiliation, hunger and poverty. But still they felt they could persevere.

This kind of life only contributed in making my grandma Lencha a tough woman. My grandmother often told me if she had been through all this in her childhood and survived, anything else life threw at her was a piece of cake. Now the matriarch of her own brood, she was determined to apply this same attitude into all of us. She knew how to push us. We were blood of her blood and she expected us to perform to her standards..

As I stood outside waiting for the inevitability of my punishment, I held out hope that she would be merciful to me since my mother once alluded to me that I was one of my grandmother's favorites. No such luck. I was looking at the house trying to make out shadows via the kitchen door when all of a sudden it flung open and my sister Ida the track star flew out headed in my direction.

I heard my grandmother's voice in the background "*Y traime ese cabron aqui para darle un jalon de mechas*!" In a split second, I turned and ran and the race was on. I had always wondered what my grandmother meant whenever she said she was going to give us a "*jalon de mechas.*" But at times like this I thought it best not to stick around to find out.

I sprinted down the side of the house heading towards the front. I figured I would make good time by hitting the sidewalk then turn left towards the railroad tracks. I glanced and thought to myself if I could make it across the tracks into the street on the other side, I could dart in and out of houses and lose her by climbing the fences. I looked back and saw I had a reasonable lead on my sister. All I needed was a bit of luck to make it out of this predicament. She was fast. I was smaller and could run pretty fast too but I also knew exactly what my sister was thinking.

You have to understand the deep commitment felt by us all when my grandma would give you an order. A task failed would entitle you to be the beneficiary of her anger. In my family, this was understood by one and all. Someone was going to pay for any misdeed that occurred. If you happened to be standing next to or if she called on you, two things were going to happen - a -- you were told to carry out an assigned duty that would contribute to the solution, in this case, capture me; or - b -- in the event of failure on your part you would have to come back to explain and thus bear the brunt of her anger by being pummeled, hit, pulled or go through anyone of my grandmothers other disciplinary tactics.

You paid the consequences should you not succeed. She would grab you by the ear, any ear it didn't matter, as long as it was attached to your head, and pull on it, grab you in a headlock and give you a huge *coscoron*. Now for those people who have never had the privilege of having my grandmother's bony little hand curled up into a fist and feel her knuckles pressed into your head for about thirty seconds, well, you just haven't lived.

My sister, understanding this scenario and having been the recipient of more than a few of my grandmother's *coscorrones*, was a complete and willing enforcer in the situation. She had a total understanding of the old line that goes "hey, better you than me little brother." Failure was not an option. A *coscorone* sandwich was not on her schedule today.

I misjudged her dedication to the mission assigned, forgetting how she had defeated every other girl in her age group at track meets. To her, I was just a puny little punk who was going to get his. I stole a look back to see if she would slow down any. I turned the corner in front of the house and saw the tracks were about fifty yards away. I attempted to negotiate the turn onto the sidewalk from the house. When she hit the sidewalk she went flying around the corner as if it was a straightaway course.

Right then, I knew I was in trouble. I bore down into a sprinter's stance and prayed to the good Lord that he make my feet as light as feathers and as strong as a gazelle to carry me over the tracks in some type of flying miracle. *Please God*, I prayed, *let me live to see another day*!

The train tracks were straight ahead and looked so appealing. In a dream I could hear my feet say "come on, you can make it. You're a boy and she's a girl. You're faster than her. Come on, freedom is near." I swear I heard the rumble of fear from within my gut as I neared the tracks shouting to me that I was strong and no one but NO ONE would keep me from surviving. I am the man and I will win, yeah!

The growling I mistakenly thought coming from my insides was actually the rumbling of the westbound train heading for the precise location on the tracks pegged as the target area to help me escape this crazy woman. I cannot put into words the feeling of helplessness when I realized I was not about to beat the train. Trying to beat it would be suicide, although for a moment there I thought this fate would be far better than having to face my grandmother's wrath. I stopped to look around for another escape route and actually thought for a second about jumping on the train to take me far, far away.

Just then a hand grabbed my shirt from behind in a death grip I knew I would not be able to break. The evil terminator sent to retrieve me had found its mark and was not about to let go. I turned to face my sister. She yanked me back and this allowed her to get a good grip on my arm which she now placed in a lock behind my back.

The train was whizzing by now. I felt dizzy from the hot air stream coming from the train. I could smell the metal on metal grinding together, lathered in oil. The stench pierced the air. It took me a second to gather my thoughts and try to break free of this death grip. I pulled away and immediately started running in the opposite direction towards the corner of the block. I thought I could hit the left turn street at the other end of the block. It was the only way in and out since the tracks blocked the other side. I could see my grandmother standing outside the front door screaming at my sister as we passed her house.

"*Que lo traigas aquí o a los dos les voy a dar un jalon de mechas.*" This was not good. Now, not only was I going to get a *jalon de mechas*, but my sister was now threatened with getting the same. This would only fuel her resolve in catching the evasive prey. Once she heard my grandma threaten to give both of us a "*jalon de mechas*", she put it into third gear. She took off right behind me and shifted into warp speed with the grandmother's threat ringing in her ears. I got as far as the corner and was about ready to make the turn when I felt her push me from behind. This caused me to lose my balance and tumble face first into the street. I felt the skin on my knees scraping off as I slid in the concrete. I tried to stop the skid but to no avail. I felt the pain of my fingernails digging into the pothole now staring me in the face. I slammed into the hole and hit my head as I rolled over on the street a couple of times trying to come to a stop. I felt my sister's knee in the small of my back. There were so many areas in pain that I just lay there in a battered state and surrendered.

"You're gonna get it, you're gonna get it, hah hah!" she teased as she curled her lips into this sneer. It made me shudder at the thought she was probably right. She placed me in a tight headlock, and didn't let go even when I tried to get my footing and stand up. She repeated the dreaded truth as we both headed back to the house. Even though she was being contemptuous in her mood towards me, I knew she had a sense of relief that she would not be feeling the wrath of my grandma Lencha. An action that was reserved for me.

I tried to reason with her as she walked back with me in this awkward position. I told her that if she let me go, I would do the same for her whenever she got into trouble. I promised her I would wash dishes for her when her turn came around, for the rest of her natural life. I would name my children after her. She could have anything of value in my life if she just let me go. I thought this was a fair deal considering her disposition to always getting into trouble. I really was committed to meeting my end of the bargain. I would have sold my soul to the devil just to get out of this predicament.

"Nope, no way, I'm taking you back and you're gonna get yours" she said. I prayed for mercy.

At the time, my grandma was about fifty years of age. Not too short, but medium, she was a strikingly attractive woman. I had seen pictures of her when in her twenties, she reminded me of Betty Davis, except in a darker skin tone. She had these big dark eyes, which my mother, my sisters and myself all inherited from her. She took pride in the fact that after seven children, she could still fit into the clothes she wore when she was in her twenties. Her long black hair curled down just at the right intervals which made her look younger. She had survived two husbands who had fallen in love with her large black eyes and naturally pouty lips. She had a fiery personality that evoked passion in everything she did. Today as I recall the events of this story, in my fifty years alive, I have yet to meet another woman who embraced everything in life with such passion.

She was a drinker. I recall when the family got together for celebrations, she could out drink any man or woman there. Family gatherings included us, my tio Manuel with his large clan along with my tio Fermin's crew who lived in Juarez. Even the neighborhood friends came over to celebrate, Chapenco, El Gordo, Kikirica and sometimes people I didn't even know came over but all knew and liked my grandmother. Chapenco and Kikirica were great guitar players and they would come over to play and sing corridas and rancheras. People would be singing and dancing in the front yard and my grandmother of course was the life of the party. There would be beer and food and beer and tequila and beer and beer and it was just a great party. We were duty bound to come and enjoy the festivities even though my mother didn't like it since she had given up drinking and smoking. My father was a different story. He was always ready to come and party.

I would see my father and my grandfather (her latest husband) drink a shot of tequila to celebrate whatever the occasion was. And there was my grandmother, the only woman in the group having a shot and cussing just like the men. But just like that she would go back into the kitchen and whip up massive meals of *chili rellenos and sopa and caldo de pollo and menudo and tamales.* Man, it makes my mouth water just thinking about all that good food. The women were expected to help out in the kitchen because my grandmother believed that a good woman could drink with her man, cook for her man and keep her man happy. This was my childhood and this was the woman I saw in my grandmother. She could do just about anything else a man can do and was damn proud of it. Not a big woman in stature, yet she demanded respect. For the life of me, I cannot recall a time when anyone did not give her that respect. She was a hard drinker and a smoker but also a superb cook and she kept an immaculate home. She was a tough person who could stay up and play poker with the men and drink all night long. In the morning, she would rise from the playing table, the other men having given up and passed out on the ground beside the table. Once they woke up, she would brew them a strong pot of black coffee and bring everyone back to their senses.

After a smoke and a couple of cups of coffee, her day of cleaning and cooking would start and after a quick nap, she came back to life not once complaining about a hangover. Everyone respected her and everyone loved her. She was and has been the toughest, yet most comforting woman I have ever been around in my entire life. Taking nothing from no one but giving lots to those she loved. So here I was, eleven years old being hauled down to appear before her and bear the brunt of her fury.

# CHAPTER THREE

My sister approached my grandma Lencha like a roman soldier sent off to conquer far away lands. Returning to her emperor with conquests from the victory. I decided to cry out in excruciating pain. The various cuts and bruises inflicted on me by my slide into the street and the pain inflicted by my sister really hurt. My only hope now was for mercy. I started to scream out in a shriek of pain. "AAAYYYYY, me *duele, me duele,*" I screamed.

"*Chavalo mocoso, callate, todavía no te duele hasta que acabe contigo entonces vas a sentir dolor,*" replied my grandma. To her left was my little brother crying and holding an ice pack to his head. My grandmother had told him to place it on top of the enormous bump on his head. His head was so big to begin with it was hard to see where the head ended and the bump began. I realized this was not a time for jokes although looking at him reminded me of that episode on the twilight zone where the aliens land on earth and…

Oh forget it….

My grandmother told my sister to release her death grip. As I stood there in front of her looking at her deep dark eyes that pierced into my very soul. Trembling with fear, I remembered for a second my mother had told me that I was one of my grandmother's favorites. I clung to this small ray of hope with a sense of apprehension but it turned out to be a false omen. She quickly grabbed my left ear lobe and proceeded to pull me through the front door heading towards the back of the house. I could see my brother's face turn into a smile between sobs as he took heart knowing that the guilty party in this conspiracy was about to get his.

I was taken kicking and screaming into the back yard with both my evil enforcer sister and my two headed monster brother in tow. I could tell we were heading towards the fence separating the yard from the cemetery grounds. Along the way, my grandma Lencha picked up a discarded milk crate lying on the ground. She never really stopped to pick it up. Instead she scooped it up with one hand and held on to my ear with the other as we continued making our way to the corner fence area.

Once there, she placed the milk crate at the far corner of the fence. She then slammed my butt squarely on top of it. The crate felt hard as I was unceremoniously plunked down on it. It was a welcome relief since she finally released the grip on my ear. I sat down facing her as she started scolding me, pointing her finger at my face.

"*Y aquí te quedas y vale mas que no te muevas.*" she said. I did not move a muscle. She turned and stormed back into the kitchen with the two gargoyles in step behind her.

I stared at the kitchen door, waiting for her return with a fear of what it would bring. Perhaps she would bring a pack of wild dogs to eat me. Maybe she would come out with a hammer in hand to finish the job. Or maybe a carving knife to chop me up and feed me to the pigs as a feast. When you're eleven years old, your mind tends to wander a lot. But considering the fact my grandma was feared by both men and women in the neighborhood, one could never be sure.

The kitchen door did not open as I stared at it, wishing with all my might that it remain forever closed. Slowly, I took in my surroundings and began to think that perhaps I had withstood the onslaught. I was not that much worse for wear. Looking around I evaluated my predicament. It was late afternoon in October. A time when the desert days are comfortable but the nights bring a chill to the fall air. It was comfortable enough for a T-shirt in the daytime but a shirt or light jacket would be more appropriate for the nights.

I sat on the crate by the fence at the far corner away from the house. Behind me, the cemetery grounds were to my left and my right. The house next door had been sold the previous year and the owners of the cemetery wasted no time in buying up the property to expand their business. All the houses on Radford were set for demolition as the owners waited for the residents to either move or die off. In fact the cemetery owners would show up a couple of times a year to ask my grandmother if she was ready to sell the house. They always came in with some ridiculous price for it, or at least that's what my father always told my mother when they would talk about it. No one really cared if the offer was fair since the block was full of Mejicanos anyway. The city was not about to stand up for anybody that lived on Radford street. Even I knew that.

My grandmother would always say the house had too many memories to let it go. This is where they had first settled when she married my real grandfather. The tiny house had been home to my mother as a little girl. Often, she would tell us she remembered playing in this same backyard. The yard where I was now serving my penance.

Even though the next door neighbors had relented and taken the money the cemetery had offered, everyone knew it was only a matter of time before all the homes on the block would be bought out. Time was on the side of the cemetery owners. I found it ironic that eventually, the cemetery would swallow up the property and be home again for the people who presently occupied the land. Perhaps in the future my grandmother would wind up buried in the same spot where she had done her living.

As night began to fall, I stared at the different headstones and crosses that marked the final resting place of so many. Often I often wondered about the many different lives the persons buried there had led. By the dates on the headstones, some reflected long periods of life encompassing sixty to almost a hundred years alive. Some showed dates of children who died way before their time. Some reflected those of day old children who did not live any life at all. I didn't like to dwell on these thoughts because as I pondered the lost souls buried here, my mind would begin to drift towards ghosts and goblins and stories of "*la llorona*"

The old Mexican wives tale about a woman who lost her children in an accident. She was so distraught that she killed herself and wandered the earth crying and looking for them and…no I'm not going to think about that...I told myself. I sat on the milk crate and forced myself back into reality.

The cool night penetrated my flimsy t-shirt and thought of ghosts and spirits only contributed to the dank feelings. I tried hard to focus on how long I would sit out here and reasoned that she could not leave me out here for too long. My mother would be home soon and grandma Lencha would not be able to explain how I had frozen to death in a milk crate in the backyard by the corner of the cemetery. Or maybe that was the plan! No it couldn't be. I mean, surely there was some law that said you couldn't do this to a child. I looked around and the granite headstones seemed to stare back. With welcome tidings as if to say "soon, you will be lying here, soon you will be one of us". I could swear there were glowing lights coming up from the stones.

I closed my eyes and prayed hard to the angels placed atop some of the granite monuments, telling myself I was too young to go. I had a lot of life to live. I caught myself opening my eyes to see if there were any ghosts rising up from the headstones. The moon was out in full force now and I trembled from the cold and feared this punishment was bearing on me. I hated my grandma because I was forced to sit here and not following her orders would only lead to more physical pain inflicted on me because of my disobedience.

If I so much as showed any fear, it would only serve to anger her more. I was eleven years old and I was scared and so, I faced the end. Here in the yard, with a full moon out and me about to be swallowed by ghosts from the dead. Ready to rise up and engulf me into their world, I came to peace with it all and said goodbye to the cruel world. I was scared shitless. I stared straight ahead looking at the kitchen door which had a glow from the kitchen light turned on inside. I could see shadows of my sisters and my brother sitting down to eat dinner. I felt a sniffle in my nose. Due both to the cold and the oncoming flow of tears since I was so hurt, angry and scared.

I'll show them, I said, to myself. I'll come back and haunt them and scare them every night. I wiped away a tear from my eye as I saw my grandmother open the kitchen door and walk towards me. She had on a light green sweater that I remember being warm to the touch. When I would snuggle up and hug her, I could feel its warmth and comfort so I knew at least SHE was comfortable walking towards me.

She had a scowl on her face but as she approached me I could tell she got her first glimpse of me crying. I quickly turned away so she would not see me though I thought I noticed her frown turn upward slightly. As she walked up to me, she didn't seem so upset. She pulled up the old kitchen chair my grandfather had left outside and sat down next to me.

"*Ya sabes que hicistes mal,*" she said.

"Yes," I replied. "I know I did wrong."

"Él *es tu hermanito y tú lo tienes que cuidar,*" she said.

"Yes," I answered. "I know he's young and I'm older and I should know better."

She stood me up and made me stand in front of her. I looked into those large pools of blackness she called her eyes. She lifted my chin up so I would not look down. "*Mijo*, I want you to grow up to be a good man. I want you to be responsible and not do wrong. You are the son of my oldest daughter and I do not want you to grow up to be a problem like your brother David."

My grandmother was referring to my older half-brother, born to my mother when she was only sixteen. He was fifteen years older than me and was always getting into trouble with the law. As a teenager, he was always in and out of juvenile homes. My mother and grandmother would always worry a lot about him. One time when the sheriff's deputies came to tell my mother he had been picked up for stealing, I remember my mother going over to the kitchen window after they left with tears in her eyes. My grandmother had gone over to console her as my mother stared out the window. My mother said "*no se que hacer*" (I don't know what to do with him!).

They would talk in whispers. My grandmother would then dress and go with her to get my brother out of the detention center. A few days later they would appear before some gringo judge who would always tell her the same story. He would give my mother a chance this time but if he's caught causing trouble again, it would mean jail time. My mother would bring us along since my grandmother was babysitting us but since she didn't understand a lot of English, my grandmother couldn't tell us what was going on. My oldest sister would always explain what was happening. She was told to watch us and sit in the back of the courtroom and keep us quiet or we would all get a "jalon de mechas" (there's that word again) from my grandmother.

My sister probably thought that explaining things to me might keep me interested but it never did. I wanted to go out into the hall and play with the other kids who were there with their parents, waiting their turn to appear before the magistrate. All of us were Hispanic, all of us poor. Now sitting here before my grandmother and listening to her talk to me about my brother, I thought about all those times we had gone to the court. How my mother and my brother would cry. I thought about myself doing that to her. I didn't want to make my mother cry.

"Do you understand *mijito*, why I want you to be a good boy?" My grandma Lencha was not very good at English so when she did try and speak it, there was probably a special reason for it. I looked into her eyes and nodded up and down.

"Yes, I understand what you want me to do," I answered her.

She smiled at me and hugged me into her shoulders. "*Asi es mi hijito,*" she said. I felt her warmth in my bones. Just as I thought my punishment was over, she yanked me back by my shoulders and stared me in the eye. "*Ahora, siéntate aquí por un ratito más y luego puedes venir a comer, yo te hablo de la puerta. Me entiendes*!"

"Yes," I meekly responded. Although I didn't understand why I still had to sit out here for a little while longer. I later understood that she wanted to get her point by scaring me into staying the straight course. I will call you to come inside and eat but for now, think about what you did and understand that it was wrong, she had ordered.

"Si abuela" I replied as I sat on the crate again. I stared down at the base of the crate and I could see her feet as she stood up to leave. I didn't know what she was doing standing there but I felt her warm green sweater wrap around my shoulders and chase away the cold from the chilly air. She didn't say anything and still had a stern look on her face. I looked up at her but without saying a word, I smiled and showed her how thankful I was for this small reprieve. Not a word was spoken but our eye contact was enough to let me know she still loved me and my look reflected gratitude at this small gesture.

She turned and walked away leaving me to fend for myself against the demons of the cemetery while at the same time showing me that she was with me in my personal battle. It was one of those times in life when the punishment, the example and the lesson all rolled into one moment. I was being punished for my actions since she knew that sitting an 11 year old boy in the dark next to a cemetery on a moonlit night was enough to scare me straight.

As I look back now and as she later told me before she passed away, I realized she was trying to make me a stronger person. Now granted, some people may call this extreme punishment. But I understood my grandmother. She was the type of person who was tough with a caring side to her. On the outside she could be the toughest person to anyone who met her for the first time. If you treated her with respect and if you showed her the real you and weren't out to screw her for anything, she would give you the shirt off her back. She wanted us to be good people. She wanted us to learn to stand up for ourselves in this world. She knew how cold and cruel this world could be. She also knew that love was a very important part of a person's life. Toughness and love would balance each other out. One side would keep the other one on an even keel. To her, this was the definition of a good person.

"You must be tough to protect yourself and those around you from the evils of this world," she would always say. "But you must also learn to give of yourself. Do not intimidate but do not be intimidated. Do not cross others unless they cross you first. And if you commit to this life, let it be that you are true to yourself and others will respect you for it. When you find someone who is genuine with you, be genuine to them. This is the basis for a good life and a basic element of love." She would always say this when she was in a mood to talk, usually while smoking her pall malls with a rum and coke on the table by her side. She would get tipsy and put her feet up to her side, sitting on the sofa to talk to us.

My siblings and I would be running around playing, but sometimes I would listen to the conversations between her and my mother. I was old enough to understand some things and too young to understand others. In those instances, I would go back to playing with my cousins or my brother. But sometimes, I would understand and my grandmother would pick me up and sit me next to her. When she had on that green sweater, I would cuddle up next to her and listen to stories about when she was a little girl in Mexico or what happened to her the day before or why she had married three times or really just anything. I felt comfortable in her arms and she always made it a point to sit me with her. She would always tell my mother I would be different. When my mother would say I was too young to understand anything, my grandmother would disagree and tell her that I understood more than what she thought.

"*De todos tus hijos, este va ser muy diferente*" she would say. I did grow up to be different from my other brothers and sisters for I understood the intricacies of the lessons from my grandmother. Right then, in the backyard, all I knew was I was sitting out in the dark next to dead bodies. But I was not as scared as I had been before. I was entrusted with a feeling of ease and comfort knowing that my grandmother expected me to be OK. She didn't worry about me because I was her grandson and perhaps there was a certain specialty that came with that. Maybe she knew something I didn't. Maybe she saw something in me or maybe she instilled into me this strong sense of will into me that was in our blood. After all, I was blood of her blood or maybe she just believed in me. Either way, I sat there feeling that quite frankly, I was going to be alright. There would be no demons coming to take me away. There would be no ghosts trying to pull me down into the murky depths. I was going to be OK because she was my grandma and she told me so. And I believed her.

I leaned back on the chain link fence and looked up at the full moon that glowed a shadowy light that covered the vast area in front of me. I had a sense of well-being. I felt as if someone was going to help me grow in this journey of life and act as a sort of mentor to me. I was a willing student and I felt obliged to listen to the directions about to be given. I picked up some small rocks lying nearby and started to throw them at the different tombstones around me. So far, the night didn't seem so bad after all.

# CHAPTER FOUR

In the fall of 1969, the world had again turned very different. Maybe because I had turned 14 years of age and was beginning to come into my own but I now saw things around me in a vastly different light. The crazy and turbulent 60's were over and I remember that the seventies were bringing a promise of relief from the anger and confusion of the last decade. In 1968 when Martin Luther King and then Robert Kennedy were killed and the riots were going on, I felt as though the world was coming to an end. Here I was growing up in an El Paso barrio where things were oppressive enough. I thought that something must really be wrong with the world if a young Chicano *mocoso* like me was taking note of all the screwed up things going on. It seemed as if no one cared about anything except to shout louder than the person next to them. Everyone complained or was pissed off at someone or at something and they wanted everyone to know about it.

But life went on, and so I decided that if the world was truly coming to its fateful conclusion, then I might as well have a good time before I go. So in 1969, three of my buddies and I decided to go to California and see Jimi Hendrix play at the Monterey Pop Festival. My buddy Tacho and his family lived down the street from me. Originally his family had moved to El Paso, Texas from California. They were migrant workers who traveled between Texas and California picking the harvest crops during the seasons. His mother had developed a case of bad allergies in California and the doctors there had recommended a drier climate. So his father decided to bring the family to a home base between the Texas valley and the fields of California.

They lived on Macias street in the barrio. During harvest time, the kids and the father would drive either north or south, depending on the time of year to pick onions, lettuce or cotton in Texas or strawberries and avocados in California.

His older sister would stay with their mother and with the little ones left at home. Tacho and I had become friends at school since the third grade. During the ages of 12 through 16, young boys come to believe there is nothing they can't do, nothing they can't accomplish and that each is invincible. And so it was with this feeling of invincibility that me, Tacho, Frankie and Tony decided to go hear the artist being hailed as the greatest guitarist in the world.

My oldest sister had been dating this guy who owned a copy of the *Jimi Hendrix Experience* and since he was trying to make points with my sister, I asked him to lend it to me. We would play the tape on the old 8 track system that we had stolen...I mean…, bought at the local Western Auto store on Montana street. We kept it out in the tool shed that Tacho's dad had built behind the house. There, we listened to music and it gave us a place to mellow out. His father had so much junk in there, he didn't know what was where. Since Tacho had been out to California and we hadn't, we all hatched this idea that we could stay with his tia in San Jose. Tacho would talk his cousin Fito into going up to San Francisco with us to the concert. Fito was eighteen and he was really into the San Francisco music scene. Since I had only been to Los Angeles with my parents on the train to visit my cousins in East LA, I had no idea where San Jose or San Francisco were.

All I knew was that if we could jump the train by Memorial Park in central El Paso we would get a free ride to California. This was the boldness in us talking. We could go to the concert and spend the nights with Tacho's cousins in San Jose and come back with his father and his older brothers who were picking grapes in Fresno. I thought we had everything figured out and I planned to tell my parents that I was going on vacation to Fabens, Texas with Tacho and his mother to visit his aunt who lived there. We would only be gone for a couple of days. We were to say that his father and mother were going and that they had invited me along.

Trouble was, his mother was a casual friend of my mothers and occasionally they would see each other at the bingo hall down at the community center. I thought they might see each other during the time we were gone but I gambled that they wouldn't. We were only talking about being gone five days at the most. We left on a Thursday night and caught a westbound train leaving for Phoenix where we would get off and jump onto one bound for San Francisco. My mother went to bingo that Friday night and just my luck, she was surprised to see Tacho's mother playing bingo two tables over. When she noticed her there, she went over to her and the whole plan went to hell. The four of us got pulled off the train in Phoenix not because anyone from the families tried to stop us, but because the Southern Pacific police were checking box cars and they came across four Chicanos on a westbound train that they thought were Mexican illegals trying to catch a ride west to California. They threatened to have us deported to Mexico unless we gave them our true identities.

Once we came clean as to who we were, they called the police in El Paso who called our parents who decided to drive seven hours to Phoenix to pick us up. Frankie Munoz, one of the guys with us, had a father who owned a semi-truck that he contracted out and he offered the other fathers a chance to go with him to Phoenix to pick us up. Of course on the way back, we had to sit in the back of the truck with the crates of spare parts he was hauling from Phoenix to El Paso. In those days, trucks weren't checked as frequently at checkpoints as they are now and he left the door partially open so we could get some air into the back.

When the fathers initially showed up to get us in Phoenix, we explained to them why we were initially heading out to California. We hoped that their sense of youthful adventure and the fact we were all men would be reason enough to explain the daring exploits of being young and wanting to explore your wild side. It didn't seem to do any good. We all got a beating from each father right there in the parking lot of the juvenile facility in Phoenix where we had been held overnight. Each father had taken custody of his son and had given each a good whipping before placing us into the tractor trailer. The Phoenix cops got a good laugh at seeing each boy get a whipping and as we pulled out of the parking lot with us sitting on top of the crates with the back door open. We flipped the cops off with a bird which caused them to pull Franky's dad over which led to us being whipped again which led to us being put back on the truck a second time heading back to El Paso.

Man, I was never so happy to leave Arizona as that particular day. When we got to El Paso, my father told me not to try anything that stupid again. The next day on Sunday, we went to grandma Lencha's house to celebrate her 54th birthday party. I thought I would get a lecture from my mother and grandmother since my mother immediately told my grandmother about the adventures from the day before and how she had been so mad at me for having pulled such a stunt. I didn't know how my grandmother would react but I knew she would not make such a big deal of it as my mother. As a matter of fact, I thought if anyone would appreciate the sense of adventure involved, it would be her. Still, my mother had made a big deal about it and I wasn't quite sure what she would say.

# CHAPTER FIVE

Since it was my grandma's birthday I knew everyone would be drinking and celebrating. I didn't think much of it. I stayed outside with my cousins from Los Angeles who had come into town with my aunt and uncle to celebrate my grandma Lencha's birthday. My uncle Tony was married to Lola who was my mother's sister. My uncle Tony loved to drink and play guitar and he loved my grandma Lencha.

She was, he said, the only woman who could out drink him when they would do tequila shots. After a few beers, my tio would challenge her to do shots and see who could stand more. My uncle would stop at four and my grandmother would stop at five. They would promise to do it again an hour later but when the hour was up, my tio Tony was standing up drunk over by the corner in the front yard singing Mexican songs to my tia Lola and expressing his love for her. They never got around to doing shots again until real late at night and even then, she could always drink more than he would. He loved to come to El Paso to celebrate my grandma's birthdays because everyone always had a lot of fun.

They always drove to El Paso, five kids and two adults and they would make it in twelve hours straight. I liked having them come see us because I knew everyone was going to be drinking and partying and everyone would be in a good mood. I was outside talking to my cousin Lily when I saw my grandmother come outside and offer my father a beer. He was on the other side of the yard talking to my tio Tony asking him about the drive to El

Paso. She talked briefly to both of them and she headed over to where I was standing.

"*No seas tan pendejo hijito,*" she said and she kissed me on the forehead as if to say, "hey glad to see you're alive and safe but boy that was pretty stupid." She walked away and my cousins laughed at me while I turned a bright colored red from embarrassment.

My LA cousins seemed a breed apart from our Texas upbringing. They brought with them this cool attitude. They kept up with the latest styles and they talked the latest smack. Everyone that lived in El Paso had cousins living in California. In fact, the way we all understood it, in the early days when our people migrated from Mexico to this country, many from that generation arrived in El Paso because of the close proximity to the border and to be with or search for family and friends escaping the civil war in Mexico.

In our ancestral family, my maternal great grandparents came to this country with eleven of their children already having been born. They crossed the border and my great grandfather found work on one of the large farms in the lower valley of El Paso that belonged to the Parker family. At the time, the valley was home to large farm lands that grew everything from onions and lettuce to cotton and cattle. The Parker farm was one of the oldest tracts in the valley and the family hired on and worked the land for over ten years. From the stories my grandmother told me, the family had prospered. She remembered these as good times as the family grew to eighteen in all. Actually my great grandmother had borne twenty-one children but three had died since midwifery was not half as competent as it is nowadays and a lack of medical expertise and disease took its toll. Still, seven sisters and eleven brothers was quite a brood.

The men were expected to help the father tend the fields and take care of the ranch and the women cared for the domestic needs. They had done so well there that Mr. Parker had made my great grandfather ranch foreman by the eleventh year there on the ranch. My grandmother says the family thought they would remain on the farm and branch off into their own piece of farming land after a few years. Old man Parker entrusted a lot of responsibility to his foreman and my great grandfather had told my great grandmother that he had promised them a large acreage of land if he would remain with him permanently. He told him not to worry about his future since his loyalty would be rewarded and his family didn't have to worry about anything for generations to come.

Mrs. Parker had borne three girls, all worked on the farm but as they had grown older, The girls had shown no intention of remaining in the family business. Since the farm had run a profitable cattle business with lettuce, onion and cotton growing supplements, the family had been well off enough to send the girls to fine schools in Dallas and Houston. Each had met a local boy whose ambitions did not include relocating to the dull valley life of farming outside El Paso. Mr. Parker had understood that his family tradition would not continue through the next generation and thus decided to break the farm into parcels and leave the land to his most dedicated employees, those who had been with them the longest and had served him faithfully all these years. Trouble was, Mrs. Parker died in her fifties from tuberculosis and thus left Mr. Parker a distraught and lonely man. He met a woman whom he thought would fill the void of his devoted wife Emma of forty-two years but it was not to be.

This new Sra. Parker was a vile woman who treated the hired help as *Mexican wetbacks* not to be trusted. She had a mean streak about her and pretty much manipulated Mr. Parker into doing anything she wanted. Things on the farm had changed and my grandmother's family did not feel as welcome and secure as in the beginning. Still, they endured in the hopes of getting their own land to farm and keep something of tangible importance within the family nucleus.

Then one day, old man Parker up and died of a heart attack. He was a good and decent man and after the funeral service they buried him on acreage on the northwest corner of the farm, which had been in his family ever since Texas had been a Republic. The widow Parker then told my great grandfather that their services would no longer be required. He told her about the agreement that he and Mr. Parker had arranged over the land grant. She would hear none of it. She demanded proof of this so-called agreement but nothing had ever been written down.

In those days, a handshake was all you needed. But the second Sra. Parker was not like the first one at all and her intent was to sell the farm in its entirety and move to Dallas. Up to the last days of his life, my great grandfather had always believed that if Emma Parker had outlived her husband, she would have honored the agreement set between him and Mr. Parker and if so, perhaps our lives would have been so much different. I always think of that when I remember that story.

So once again, the family was forced to move on and they decided to move into the then small town of El Paso where my great grandfather found work as a boot maker. This is where he worked until his untimely death at sixty-one. When he died, it fell upon my grandmother's oldest brother Francisco to be the head of the family. This was the early part of the century and El Paso was a sleepy little town whose biggest claim to anything was that Pancho Villa had crossed the river and attacked Columbus, New Mexico up the road a ways.

General Black Jack Pershing who at the time was stationed at the garrison in Ft. Bliss in El Paso had been sent by the president himself to chase Villa into Mexico and make him pay for this. Weary of the effects of the Mexican war and the ensuing poverty cast on the border areas because of it, my great uncle Francisco had decided to go out west with his brother Carlos and his sister Toya to try their luck in California.

At that time, good jobs were to be had in California and the plan was to try and make it out there while the other older sisters Petra and Serafina would remain behind with my great grandmother to provide for her and take care of the clan. But such a large family called for more working hands to provide food for everyone so one of the other brother and sister teams

(Tencha and Oswaldo) got jobs with the Union Pacific railroad company which was laying track across the country to connect the west to the east. Oswaldo brought along his brother Mario and they worked side by side with the Chinese workers hired to lay track. Tencha brought along her sister Maria and her little sister Lencha, my grandmother, who was roughly twelve years old at the time but old enough to work and contribute to the family pool.

These were the stories that fascinated me about my grandmother. At her home with her drink and her pall malls close by, I would sit and listen to her recount all these stories from her childhood. To me, it was as if history was coming to life. These were stories of the people that built this country. The U.S. had not yet entered into the First World War and therefore was still not yet a great power. I found it fascinating that at one time, we were part of the fabric that made up the small threads of this young country. Like the Italians and the Irish and the other Europeans on the east coast, the Mexicans and the Chinese and Native Americans on the west coast were positive contributing factors. As I sat there, it was as if a portal into the past had opened and I viewed it through the eyes of someone who had been there. There were no child protection labor laws yet and so the age of twelve was considered old enough to be considered a wage earner rather than another hungry mouth to feed.

She told me that at first, she was excited because it felt as if she was going away on an adventure. Seeing new things always intrigued her. Besides, she had been used to getting up and moving on someplace. To her it seemed that's what they kept doing every few years. Only difference this time was that her mother would not be making the trip and she would miss her. I remember a tear would form in the corner of my grandmother's eyes whenever she mentioned her mother. The longing for her had never really gone away after all these years. It was one of those times I would see my grandmother's tender side and this endeared me to her. Not very many people got to see my grandmother cry but I had.

Her youthful journey had led her to work on the railroads for seven years starting as a cook's assistant and working up to cook. She was responsible for helping feed the hundreds of laborers working on the great railroad. She told me that this experience had toughened her up since she grew up in a world full of men.

This is where she learned to play cards and hustle the young Chinese workers who were very good at card games. This is where she first learned to drink with hard drinkers who would earn their checks on Saturday and spend the majority of it in drunken stupors by Sunday nights. Here was a twelve year old girl growing up among hard working, hard drinking men who lived for today and didn't much care about tomorrows. Most were single, a few had families back home because as tough as it was to be apart, the railroads paid good money. Everyone worked hard and they let off steam by way of good Irish whiskey from back east or tequila from Mexico. Sometimes the Chinese workers made their own concoctions in their makeshift pots.

She felt protected by her older brothers and sisters and the family members all shared a tent together and followed her brother Oswaldo's lead. He and Tencha took care of the others and they would make do by saving and controlling the money. Still they found a way to send a little something home to El Paso and help the family out. They set up and took down camps as they traveled like nomads from outpost to outpost.

My grandmother recalled how her mother would tell stories about what it was like traveling in a circus, going from town to town, city to city and she said she could relate to being a drifter. It was a hard life yet she always told me that it proved to be the best educator for her. She learned much more about men than any home life could ever teach her. She learned what made them strive to achieve and what made them quiver like little boys. She learned about triumph and loneliness and how many times they go hand in hand. She would feed them, drink with them, flirt with them and when they tried to take advantage of her, she learned how to beat them at their own game.

She lived this life for seven years and by the time she turned nineteen, she'd had enough.

At eighteen she met a Mexican laborer who came to work the railroads from his hometown in Chihuahua, Mexico. They had fallen in love and gotten married. Soon after, she announced she was pregnant from this union. A baby girl was born and they named her Anita after his grandmother back in Chihuahua.

After my mother Anita was born they both agreed to work one more year to save up enough money to help them start a home life back in El Paso. Since they traveled around the country so much, my mother had been born in Pennsylvania, right outside Pittsburgh as the railroads were making their push back west again. The year was 1926, the depression was still three years away and generally life was good with not a hint of the bad times yet to come.

Out west in California, her oldest brother Francisco and the family sect had done well working in the orange fields and helping to build the new metropolis soon to be known as Los Angeles. Work was plentiful and some of the siblings in El Paso were anxious to get away from the redundancy of poverty prevalent in the town at the time. Francisco was gradually sending for some of them but only when he knew he could guarantee them a job with someone on a construction site or at some textile factory or something, anything that guaranteed a working chance at a new life in California. My great grandmother was getting older and he wanted to bring her out west with him also. At the time, LA extended out only to what is now known as the Boyle Heights area on the east side.

But my great grandmother was from the old country and one of her daughters Serafina had married a man from Ciudad Juarez who moved her back across the border to Mexico. Being one of the older ones, Serafina was also one of the feistier ones. She had nixed the idea of sending her mother out to California arguing that the center of the family base should remain in Texas. The matriarch was located here and thus the base of the family should remain intact, located next to the old country in El Paso. There was always friction on this matter since some wanted to stay in the El Paso/Juarez area and some wanted to follow the money out west. Out of respect for my great grandmother, Francisco adhered to the El Paso location and focused on bringing only those with the desire to go west. Serafina and two of her sisters were adamant about remaining in El Paso but generally the rest moved westward in search of a better life.

It was during this period of time that my grandmother returned to the family base in El Paso from working the railroads. She was older now, wiser than her twenty years of age would reflect. She was tough and had the shrewdness of having learned to care for herself since a very young age. Her older sister Serafina quickly took her under her wing and both sisters became a formidable part of the family hierarchy.

Anyway, we were celebrating my grandmother's birthday and the excitement of my ill fated attempt to go see Jimi Hendrix was fast approaching old news status. I decided to hang around with my LA cousins and find out the latest on things out west. Since they lived in California, they of course followed the trends associated with being Chicano in the 70's. My girl cousins wore their black hair parted in the middle and let it flow back like some Mayan goddess. They wore makeup that was pretty thick and consisted of dark makeup around the eyes giving them that popular chola look of the time. Their fingernails were done in black nail polish and they wore jeans with a typical pull over blouse like the other Southern California *cholas*.

The guys were all down wearing khaki pants and flannel shirts with no buttons done except the one at the very top around the neck. This was the Califa look made popular by Cheech Marin in the movie "Up In Smoke" and they followed it to a tee. Sometimes a white T-shirt with a bandana scarf would complete the ensemble but usually, it was the one button shirt with the shirt tail sticking out, khaki pants and black pointy shoes. They were all into the music of El Chicano, WAR, and Santana who were then making music that screamed out their proud Chicano heritage. The times also called for the required "oldies" songs made up mostly of melodies designed to keep you slow and low while cruisin'.

Yeah, it was different, it was hip and if that's what they were into at the time, more power to them. This was the time of lowriders, cruisin and making out. LA was the center of the brown soul movement. They always had good music and good stories to bring when they traveled to Texas. When they came down, everyone would look forward to getting together at my grandma Lencha's because everyone knew she threw a hell of a party. There was good food, good music, dancing, drinking, occasional fights (more than not) police calls, and arrests. A typical family get-together.

We were *familia*, descendants of the original Villagran eighteen and my grandmother was the one everyone admired. Stories of her lust for life were well known by all and just as I found her to be a fascinating person, so did the others. It seemed that each family clan had a story about her and what she did at a party or how they couldn't believe how much stamina she had or how everyone thought she was the coolest aunt. When she threw a party, everyone wanted to be there because she made it an event. There was always something going on and let's face it, it was a family event.

Somehow, my grandma Lencha was always the ringmaster and nothing happened without her knowing, approving or directing it to happen. Her authority was the final word and everyone abided by this. She was granma or Lencha to those who were close to her or Dona Lencha to those who didn't. She was not a violent woman unless provoked. No one, and I mean no one would ever dare provoke her, at least deliberately. I recalled that on this particular birthday party, my father had called me over to help him unload cases of beer and assorted food prepared by family members from the old station wagon we used to have. He made a beer run and had also stopped over at El Gordo's house to pick him up along with his brother. They both played guitar and were two of my grandmother's favorite players.

I knew enough to know that if both Gordo and his brother were coming, it was in honor of the lady. Our neighborhood friend Kikirica who was a pretty good player himself was already there and so was my brother David with his guitar. My mother's two sisters (tia Aurora and tia Fina) were in attendance along with my other uncle who lived in El Paso. It would have been considered disrespectful for all my grandma's children not to be there for her fiftieth birthday. My tia Fina lived in San Francisco and my tia Aurora who lived in Los Angeles knew that an absence at this event would lead to castigation from the family and besides they enjoyed coming in to see their mother. The congregation of musicians coupled with all the important family members being present led me to the conclusion that this would be a party for the ages.

I was with my tia Aurora's bunch when my father called me over to help him. The beer was stacked on the side of the house next to the huge buckets the adults used for parties. You could easily fit two cases of beer in there, drowning them in ice and when the beers were pulled from inside, it was ice cold to the touch. At least this is what I was told. I , of course, was too young to be sneaking off to the back yard and jumping the fence into the cemetery to drink a can of beer and anyone who says they saw me do it was lying or not yet drunk enough. My cousins and I, being around fourteen years old, would sit in the old cemetery on the same milk crate used by my grandmother a couple of years before to teach me my lesson. But I was on thin ice from the Phoenix incident so I thought better of it so I kept trying to persuade my LA cousins to act as beer thieves instead of me.

I was helping my father remove the boxes of beer from the car when I noticed three older teenage pachucos walking down the street towards my grandma's house. They were unknown to my father or me. I could tell by his look of worry that he and I both suspected they might be looking for trouble. Inside the front yard within the confines of the brick fence, people stopped and looked over at the approaching trio. The barrio that we were in was known as "LA ROCA" and then as now, there were many gang turf wars going on. In those days, guys fought with fists and knives. No one used a gun unless it was absolutely necessary because the street rules then called for real men to fight with their fists and not with guns. Anyone can shoot a gun but it takes guts to face someone down and beat the holy crap out of each other. Today, everyone's a tough guy with a gun.

They were an unfamiliar threesome with trouble on their minds and something was going to happen. My grandma was a respected person even by the local gangland hierarchy. My older brother David ran around with some of the guys from La Roca and my uncle knew most of the older gang veterans or the *veteranos* as we called them. But these guys were unknown to anybody and this was cause for concern. Like a flash my grandmother headed for the front gate and approached the three twenty somethings with long hair in khakis and t-shirts, tattoos emblazoned on their arms. My uncles, eight of the male neighbors, my father and my cousins and myself all fell in line behind my grandmother, she was the authority and we were there to back up her play.

"*Que quieren aqui*?" she asked the group in her staunch manner, arms folded across her chest and drawing a line in the sand. The three stopped in their tracks at being accosted so fervently by this five foot three inch woman with a whole herd of men behind her. Suddenly, the look of fear and concern shifted to the three pachucos.

"*Venemos a buscar a la que le dicen Lencha*". They had come looking for my grandmother.

"*Pues ya la ayaron y que*?" They had found who they were looking for and now she placed her hands on her hips, daring them to show their next move.

The lead guy with the *pachuco* cap and the dark sunglasses smiled and showed a mouth with two gold teeth in front that I would have guessed had been knocked out in some fight and replaced with the shiny gold. "*Pues yo soy el hijo de JJ, el shingon de Juárez y le traigo esto de mi jefito que se está pasando un tiempo en la pinta*".

OK, so the guy says he is the son of some guy named JJ from Juarez who is presently doing time in prison. We were all still edgy since we didn't know whether to take this as a good thing or a bad thing.

"*Dice mi jefito que le manda esto con todo salud.*" The second guy reached around behind his back and for a second I swear I heard the distinct sound of pistols being cocked coming from the area behind me where my brother and cousins were sitting. For a split second, everyone was tense and time seemed to stand still.

The second *pachuco* slowly brought his hand back around and produced a large bottle of Tequila Sauza Oro which even now is considered high quality tequila. Now no doubt these guys did NOT have the means with which to purchase such an expensive liquor on their own so how they got it was not the point here. It was accepted with the intent with which it was given, as a personally delivered gift from a past friend of my grandmother from a long time ago.

The *cholo* gave the bottle to the *pachuco* with the hat on who had identified himself as the son of JJ, whoever that was. "*Con mucho saludos en estos* días."

Again, I swear I heard the click of pistols being placed back into hidden holsters somewhere behind me. Everyone seemed to let out a sigh of relief except for my grandmother who just looked at the bottle and with hands still on hips, glared at  the bottle then to the eyes of this son of JJ. She spoke in a stern and steady voice

"*Cuando vengan aquí a mi casa, carguense con respeto a sus mayores.*" Everyone froze. She obviously had not appreciated the way these three hoods had come into a neighborhood, unknown and approaching a party full of her people in a threatening throw down attitude. This behavior could be misinterpreted and get a lot of people unnecessarily shot. She expected visitors to her house to be mindful and respectful of her and not yell out her name from the street as they had done.

The son of JJ suddenly erased the smile from his face and didn't know quite what to make of this woman standing in front of him. He suddenly realized she was not someone to be disrespected. His father JJ was some hotshot criminal across the border in Juarez and he was doing life for murder at the State prison in Texas, convicted of having skinned a man alive because he had reneged on a bet. He had been a regular at the bar where my grandmother had worked and they had become fast friends way before he became a kingpin. He had made the typical male advances to her which she had rebuffed but through the years, they had remained friends and he had not forgotten that today she turned the golden age. He had tasked his son to bring a gift to pay homage to the woman on her birthday and the son suddenly realized why his father had spoken so highly of her. He had called her a woman that was not to be trifled with. For a second, his lips turned down and his eyes gave a look that said I don't quite know whether she's going to hit me or whether

I take the bottle back. It was awkward because he was holding the bottle out for her to take. Suddenly she broke into a smile and grabbed the bottle with both hands, one cupping the bottom and the other wrapping around the guy's firm grip on the bottle.

*"Pero si es de mi amigo JJ, entonces esta vez te lo perdono,"* she said. A sigh of relief appeared on the son of JJ's face, he smiled with an ease at finally coming to a breakthrough in this standoff . The rest of us breathed a little better too.

"Orale" he said, "mis respetos Senora" and with that he acknowledged that perhaps courtesy would have been a more appropriate method of approaching the house.

He understood now that all that was required was a simple level of respect in recognition of this woman. He conceded to the lesson that had been so direct. My grandmother smiled again as she took the bottle from his hands and put her arm on his shoulder to invite them in to enjoy some food and drink. After the three couriers had a look at my LA cousins along with my brother and some of his assorted friends, the San Francisco crew from my other aunt and various family members who had not appreciated their approach either, they thought twice about it. They graciously declined her invitation and turned to walk back out of the neighborhood block before the sun went down.

In that neighborhood, once the sun went down you really shouldn't be caught walking down the street unless you were from there. Gangland turf was an important controlling factor between neighborhood toughs. During the day, unknowns from other parts of town were allowed in since various families had relatives come and visit. This was a truce observed by the different groups and there was an unspoken gentleman's agreement that this would be allowed. Once the sun went down, all bets were off. The locals knew my grandma Lencha and recognized the faces of neighbors, nieces and nephews and other family members so we were safe at her house. Some of the barrio toughs even stopped by to wish her a happy birthday and share a beer. It was understood that this was more of a family event and they respected that. Funny, in my whole life I only saw this type of behavior when it came to my grandmother.

I learned that respect is to be earned and not just given. Like the three pachucos who brought the bottle of tequila and who were now long gone, it never ceased to amaze me how I could look at barrio guys who put the fear of god into anyone suddenly become so humble and respectful in the presence of my grandmother It was a sign of respect by those around her. Although I had grown up here and really didn't know any better, this was a bad neighborhood. Someone was always getting stabbed, someone had their house broken into and the cops didn't even come in at night to patrol those streets (once the sun went down if something happened in that barrio and you needed a cop, you were on your own ).

As long as I can remember, no one ever broke into her house. I had seen her chastise some of the barrio toughs telling them not to waste their lives, to get their life together and get off the drugs. At the same time, she always asked about their mothers and fathers, asked them if they were doing OK, showing them she cared for each of them. At times, even offer them a plate of food if she saw them strung out on something just to get them down off their high. My mother always worried about her and constantly tried talking her into moving out of the neighborhood. She would tell her to take the money offered by the cemetery group and buy a home closer to us. This always struck me as strange because our neighborhood was no better off and I could not understand why my mother wanted to take her from one to another just as bad. We were certainly no better off and the only benefit I saw was that she was closer to us since we all wallowed in the same oppressive surroundings.

My grandma always dismissed my mother's pleas by waving her hand at my mother saying "*estoy bien aqui, Anna, no tengas apuro.*"

My father and I now returned to unloading the boxes of beer and food supplies from the car and he saw how I, along with everyone else, had been concerned with my grandmother's confrontation. This could not always be a good thing and sometime in the future, not everyone would concede to my grandma's will. She was, after all, a woman in her fifties. The streets could be very unforgiving and sooner or later, she might come across someone who didn't care if she was a tough cookie or not. A bullet is the only thing some of the more evil misfits in the streets know. My father noticed the look of concern on me as I watched my grandma Lencha walk back towards my brother David who with guitar in hand, waited to receive the word from her to get the music started.

"You worry about your abuela don't you?" asked my father. I shrugged my shoulders in an affirmative nod. We loaded up the last of the beer cases next to the tub of ice and started putting some into the cold ice water.

"Sometimes I'm afraid one of these guys will push back harder and she might get hurt," I said.

My father pulled the tab off a cold beer and sat on the side steps beside the house. "Let me tell you a story about how I came to know your grandmother" he started. "Way long ago when I first met your mother, your grandmother had left her first husband, your original grandfather, because he was a real *cabron* with her. He mistreated her and didn't really provide any financial support to the family. Your mother doesn't really like to talk about him and she bears a lot of anger towards him for some of the things he did. Hell, I married her and she doesn't even talk to me about certain things so I don't ask unless she wants to talk. Anyway, your grandmother threw him out of the house and she worked tending bar over at Chayo's down on Alameda street. There she met Fidel, her second husband. By this time, your mother and I had gotten married and we just had your two older sisters.

Now, when Lencha and Fidel met, they were two very similar people. He liked to party and enjoy himself, be around a lot of people you know kind of be the life of the party just like your grandmother." He pointed over to my grandma Lencha who was already breaking into a chorus of Mexican ranchera songs. "*Estoy en el Rincón de una cantina,"* her voice started to rise above the sounds and noises of a large crowd gathered around her.

"Anyway," continued my father as he took a swig of beer. "Fidel and your grandma, well, I always felt they were trying to one up each other in everything they did. You know, they always tried to talk over each other, they would each argue any point, never carried on a conversation, always seemed to be yelling at each other, always competing, you know. They had too much of the same personality for them to be considered a couple, sabes? Well, one day your grandmother comes over to our house and she's bleeding from her lip. Her face looked puffy and she said that her and Fidel had gotten into this fight and that Fidel hit her. Your mother helped her clean up and she spent two days with us to give Fidel a chance to cool down. Your mother wanted her to stay with us and not go back. Lencha would have none of that. On the third day, your grandma called and an old friend of hers named Carmela. Carmela has a daughter named Monica who at that time was in her twenties and very, very pretty. Your grandmother and Carmela come up with this plan where Monica is going to bump into Fidel down at Chayos bar and start talking and flirting with him. You know, make like she likes him. She knows Fidel will go for the bait and then she'll invite him over to her house."

My father chuckled and shook his head when he told me this last part. "So what do you think your grandmother does? Her and Carmela wait out in the alley behind the house, the one by Olvera Street. They hide behind the trash cans as Fidel and Monica pull into the driveway. Monica says she feels a little bit sick and blames the booze and says she's going to throw up in the alley. She walks toward the trashcans and Fidel follows her. Once in the alley, Carmela and your grandmother jump him and begin to beat him up while Monica, who has jumped into the fracas, holds him down. All three of them start to beat him mercilessly

'C'mon *cabron*, hit an innocent woman huh, think you're tough huh, well your not so tough now *pinche wei.* Are you?" your grandmother keeps yelling at him.

My father takes another swig of his beer, "I'll tell you what *hijo*, they left that poor bastard beaten so bad that he looked like a dirty rag doll lying in the alley when they found him. After that, he never ever hit your grandmother again. Everyone found out what happened to Fidel's humiliation. Even the *cholos* here in the barrio heard about it. I'll tell you what, they learned to respect your grandmother, or fear her, or both. This place and her reputation in the family are all your grandmother has. I wouldn't worry too much about her here. Since then, I've never seen anyone else mess with her after that," said my father as he downed the last of the beer.

I knew I probably shouldn't have but I asked my father anyway, "and you, what about you? Are you scared of her?"

My father shot me one of those looks that said you shouldn't ask that question. He said, "I respect your grandmother for who she is and because of what she's gone through. I met and married her daughter and I contributed to giving her the many grandchildren that have made her so happy." My father grabbed another beer and got up to go join my grandma Lencha who was calling him to come over and join in the chorus of drunk singers.

"But remember *cabron*, she has so many grandchildren now that she won't mind if one comes up missing" and with that he gave me a *coscorone* on the top of my head. He walked off to join the others who were now breaking into that Mexican party song, *"El Rey"*, *"Yo se bien que estoy afuera, pero el dia que yo me muera, se que tendras que llorar…"*

# CHAPTER SIX

In the spring of 1972, El Paso had become one of the leading clothing manufacturing cities in the country. Wages were cheap and there was no organized labor in the city which allowed cheap abundant labor to flourish. Add to that a constant and large pool of garment workers trained in the craft coming from Mexico and it created a pool ripe for exploitation. There were close to one hundred businesses that thrived in the garment industry and the biggest manufacturer was FARAH industries with no less than six large plants in El Paso. One of these was a half mile long building located next to Interstate 10 that stretched from the Hawkins Street exit to the McRae exit. It was roughly a mile long and employed roughly around three thousand people per shift in the one plant alone.

Three full shifts operating at six days a week for 45 weeks a year. Along with its other manufacturing plants, this created contract work for support operations that helped feed the smaller supply plants throughout the city. A line of clothing products brought recognition to the city as a distributor of fine quality work along a high profile quality line of boot makers. This reflected a blue collar attitude amongst its people that was the staple of the town. This was also a time of great change within the Chicano community. Activism was awakening in the barrios in reaction to the poor working conditions and social exploitation being experienced by the textile workers in El Paso.

Out west, Cesar Chavez was leading his famous strikes against the grape growers of California giving rise to the United Farm Workers of America. Many in El Paso had relatives there or at one time, they themselves had picked the harvests of the land there as well as in Texas. The progress of the decade-long struggle for better working conditions was followed here with keen interest. In Los Angeles, a defiant group of brown berets were following the example of the socially conscious Black Panther party in Oakland. In East Los Angeles a protest turned into a riot leaving Ruben Salazar dead. Salazar was a photographer for the Los Angeles Times who had been born and raised in El Paso thus creating a tie between the tragedy and the local community. A local boy who had made good but who was killed during a demonstration against the social conditions experienced by Chicanos in California.

It was a time of struggle and elements within El Paso took note. Chicanos were trying to change things for the better for the garment workers who numbered in the thousands at the time. There was no union to watch out for the concerns of the workers forced to stand and perform on grueling eight-hour shifts. Conditions inside the factories were deplorable due to lack of ventilation and workers were not allowed to stop and rest, allowing only small fifteen minute breaks from the sweaty conditions on the plant floors. The same conditions experienced by Hispanic farm workers toiling in the hot sun picking produce were felt by the garment factory workers who were no better off. Workers were expected to perform at maximum levels in deplorable conditions. There were people who wanted to change these conditions and follow the examples being set by the Chicano activists out west.

El Paso was not Los Angeles by any means but the influx of Hispanics from this town to L.A. equated to strong ties. If there is one insecurity shared by all El Pasoans, it is that the rest of Texas never really pays proper attention to the town. Being out there by itself, the city always tried to find its own identity albeit in its dubious location across the river from Juarez. It seemed like a curse to be located here since the city never got the money to fuel its growth. Border wages were always on the low end of the meter here and thus fueled the take advantage-of-the-worker attitude among the garment companies that employed the large pool of unskilled workers.

When workers complained about working conditions, they were quickly terminated and replaced by another only too glad to accept the minimum wage due to the lack of well paying jobs in town This contributed to a constant cycle of low wage earners willing to put up with the conditions set forth by the companies.

My older cousin Nena worked at the plants. She was my tia Josefinas oldest daughter. My tia was second in line to my mother and the one rebel in the family who mirrored my grandmother's bad habits in the worst way.

My mother Anita was a quiet, unassuming person who accepted her responsibility as the oldest and who became a sort of second mother to her siblings. She was the dutiful child, always there for her mother, always concurring with her wishes, always ensuring proper behavior from the others.

My tia Josefina on the other hand was the mirror image of my grandmother's bad persona. She loved to party and drink and she smoked like her mother. She would wind up in two marriages, one to an abusive man and the other to a man with an impassive nature. She knew her way around the world of seductive charm and grace and she played it well with the men she met. She was the spitting image of my grandmother's bad side. Many times my mother and her would clash on an endless list of issues covering everything from men to cooking. They didn't really agree on too much. Both were born of the same woman and both reflected the best and the worst of her. But they had a mutual respect and understanding between each other that I would not learn about until later in my life. No one argued more with my mother than my tia, but no one else stood up more for my mother than her.

My tia Josefina had her children at a young age also and struggled to raise them when her first husband left her with two young ones. She decided to move by herself to northern California, a move unheard of at the time especially with two young mouths to feed. She lived right outside of San Francisco and made a living as a waitress at a restaurant where she worked for thirty-two years. She bought her first house a year and half after she arrived and a year later sold it at a profit. She bought another one, fixed it up and sold it again and did the same thing until she was able to afford three homes, all in her name. She had become very proud and independent. She was a shrewd woman in her financial dealings. She raised her children in the same tough way she viewed life, trust no one and depend only on yourself.

My cousin Nena, her first-born, was conceived when my tia was only sixteen. My grandmother Lencha offered to keep Nena with her in El Paso just until my tia could settle down and send for the child in California. So Nena was born to yet another woman born of struggle who also inherited the same belief in principles as her mother and her grandmother. This made for a volatile combination. Nena took a no nonsense approach to everything in life. At eighteen, she worked at the large Farah plant along the freeway in the heat and the sweat of those stifling conditions. After a while Nena thought a change of working conditions was in order and with the support of others, vowed to do so.

She started by bringing a few select workers over to the house to discuss working conditions. These workers would turn out to be the first leaders of the movement to unionize the garment industry in El Paso. These were difficult and tense times since everyone knew that any activity against the company would be dealt with immediately. Any worker caught trying to speak out against conditions would be terminated.

Since we would stay with my grandmother while my mother and father worked, I would sit and listen to plans of action that were formulated in order to get unionized. I was around sixteen years old now and the world was more in focus for me. During the meetings, my grandmother would be busy doing chores around the house. At times, she would stand off to the side of the group, arms crossed and listening while the group debated. They were compassionate people and their anger rang clear. Workers who were willing to sacrifice to effect changes.

In discussions, radical ideas were tossed back and forth but it appeared that they all seemed clueless on an initial approach. They were leaderless and although the effort was there, the leadership skills necessary to focus the group were missing. Small signs of resistance were starting to appear among them as the group searched for the one catalyst to start the movement into motion.

One day at about the third meeting held at her house, the news came that some of the workers within the group were to be terminated. Apparently someone had fingered some, but not all, of those in attendance. Immediately fingers were pointed and accusations were made by those targeted against those who were not. The meeting was turning into chaos with shouting and obscenities being hurled at each other.

When my grandmother heard the commotion and came into the room she scolded them, "*Ya basta, callense cabrones, que es la problema aquí, porque gritan*!" My grandmother then learned that half the group was to be terminated the next day and this included my cousin Nena. The group was eagerly searching for a scapegoat and without any proof had been accusing one another of being traitors.

My grandmother stood in the middle of the group and turned to face each one. She gave an impassioned speech to each person there. She said, "You all came together because you believed in the same belief. Each of you wanted to change a wrong into a right. Each of you came to rely on each other because you knew you could accomplish this together. You all knew the risks you were taking on. Now that you got caught, you look for someone to blame among you. Does anyone have proof that one of you here betrayed the rest?"

She turned and faced my cousin Nena, "Well, do you have proof of anyone here who is the traitor?" My cousin Nena who always had something to say looked down at the floor and shook her head no.

"Then stick together and finish what you started. Keep the bond strong because in the days ahead, you will need to depend on each other to make it through this." She turned and looked each individual in the eye, "But if I find out that one of you, and I don't care who it is, man or woman, if I find that one of you betrayed the others. Then so help me God, there will be no place on earth where you will be safe from me because I will find you and make you pay for what you did,"

She said as she pointed to Nena. "She is my *sangre*, blood of my blood and she took a big risk in bringing all of you together. If you hurt her, you hurt me. God may have mercy on your soul but I won't."

I had seen my grandmother threaten people before and I had seen fear in the face of those people. As I stood there and watched, I felt a chill run through my spine. Without a word she walked away from the center of the group and no one moved until she disappeared into the kitchen. They all looked at each other as they took in the message that had just been laid down. Quietly, they filed out the door without speaking, got in their cars and drove off with my grandmother's words still fresh on their minds.

Nena sat down on one of the chairs left in the semi-circle with this blank look on her face. She didn't know what to say. She had never heard my grandmother express such passion on her behalf. Sometimes in life you think you know a person and one day you realize just how deep their feelings are for you. Nena was having trouble accepting this because she had been unaware that my grandmother was full of such emotions. Beneath this hard exterior she exhibited, there was a genuine person inside who truly cared for us.

As it turned out for the group, they found that no one had been the culprit. A plant worker's wife was talking to someone at the local store and someone else heard them mention names. They told someone else who told someone else until it finally reached someone in management. Names were discussed, a list of employees was drawn up and yes, my cousin was in the group that was fired. Before they were terminated though, the group decided to reach out to the farm workers union and persuaded Cesar Chavez to come to El Paso and speak to the textile workers at a rally benefiting their desire to become unionized. After the rally, the plant workers decided to go on a strike that lasted for several months.

Management at Farah finally conceded to certain demands but still refused to unionize the members until much later when more strikes put a serious dent in production. Ultimately, the plants started closing due to the financial hit they suffered and management claimed they never recovered.

The ripple effect from the strikes led to the downfall of other plants like dominoes in a row. Eventually the union did succeed in its quest to unionize the workers but it was already too late. The huge apparel industry started going overseas or to Mexico where companies could really take advantage of cheap labor.

I never forgot the day Cesar Chavez came to El Paso. At the rally, there at the front on the stage next to him was my cousin Nena. Next to Nena was my grandmother. The local paper snapped a picture for its coverage of the strike and there on the front page was a photo of my grandmother, shaking hands with the great man. I remember it as quite a sight. Heck even before that, my grandmother walked the picket lines with the workers while she was babysitting us. We even got caught up in helping by serving water and passing out leaflets.

I admired my cousin. She had been a visible force and I admired her tenacity at sticking with the hard struggle although for a woman of her determination and upbringing, it did not surprise me. From this lesson, I learned strength and compassion on the part of my grandmother. Most grandmothers would have been in the kitchen making meals or at home doing chores. Mine was out on a picket line calling for an end to injustice. This had a profound impact on me and I can recall how she reminisced with the strikers about her own times spent working the railroads and all the abuse she was forced to endure. As she spoke I could see the look on the faces of the workers, mesmerized by her tales of perseverance just as I had been.

I recall sitting by her side feeling like her protector against any and all who would try to harm her. She noticed this and at times I think she enjoyed this protectiveness fawning over her. I had grown about five inches between my 12th and 13th birthdays and I was stretching up to a strong and tall six feet. Anytime she would go somewhere I was by her side to fetch, to call on or to help her in any way I could, there to hear her speak or chastise anyone who crossed her. She called me her *morenito* and through this we nurtured a warm and comfortable bond.

She still had her fiery side though. Once, I recall there was a traffic accident on Paisano Street where we got caught up in traffic one hot summer day. My father was driving his old 1965 Bel Air with my mother in the front seat next to him. My brother and I were in the back. Each was seated at the end by the windows to escape the searing heat since the air conditioner in the car was broken and there was no money to fix it. My grandmother was sitting between us. We were coming back from Juarez and the long wait at the international bridge to cross over to the U.S. had been especially tiring. Now there was some idiot trying to cut across the traffic lanes and avoid the backup the accident had created. This guy's car was slowing traffic so when my father's car moved forward, his driver's side came up next to my father's window.

My father, clearly upset with this guy, yells out "*Hey pinche, no estás en Juarez,*" clearly signifying that in Juarez it was OK to drive like an idiot but not on this side of the border. *Hey Buddy, you don't pull that crap over here!*. The guy leaned out the window and looked at my father while my mother pulled on my father's shirt telling him that the idiot driver wasn't worth it.

The idiot yelled back at my father "*Callate pendejo*" as he crawled by in his car still causing a mess. With that, my grandmother reaches over and pulls on the handle to open the door next to me. Once opened, she jumped over me in what seemed like an Olympic move that would have earned her a 10.0 on the scorecard.

She proceeds to walk over to this guy's window and starts whooping on him with her purse as she screams, "*El pendejo eres tu baboso, que no ves como va el pinche tráfico estúpido.* My mother screams at my father to jump out and bring her back into the car while my brother and I sit in the back seat laughing at the way the guy's head keeps rolling back and forth as the purse makes contact.

My father gets out and reaches her in the middle of traffic. thank god, was at a crawl and tried to talk her back into the car. But my grandma Lencha just keeps swinging at the guy saying, "*A quien shingados le dices pendejo cabron, el pendejo eres tu.*"

Back in the car, my mother's face has turned red from embarrassment and she smacks me in the head and tells me not to laugh. My brothers laugh louder than I did and as I tell my mother he's laughing, she smacks him in the head too. My mother gets out of the car and tells my father to grab my grandmother and put her back in the car so we can get the hell out of here. All the cars are blowing their horns, my grandmother is whaling away at the idiot who is seeing stars in his head and people are laughing as my mother keeps yelling at my father.

Finally at great personal risk, he grabs my grandmother by the waist, picks her up and carries her back to the car while she keeps yelling to no one in particular "*Ese hijo de su pinche madre, ahorita le pongo una shinga para que sepa que es shinga…*" My father opens the door next to me and throws her into the rear seat where she lands on top of me. She is still cursing as my father slams the back door and jumps into the driver's seat. My mother jumps into the passenger seat and tells my father to gun it.

My grandmother flips around and sticks her head out the window to yell at the guy who sits in his car in a comatose state from the purse whooping. He has a red spot on the side of his face in the shape of a purse. Since I'm between her and the door, she keeps spitting into my face while yelling at the guy as she leans out the window to continue her tirade, "*Bajate cabron y aquí mismo te pongo una shinga.*"

My father guns the engine and starts to drive away while my mother tries to pull my grandma back down into the middle seat. My brother is crying because grandma accidentally kicks him in the face with her shoe as she tries to lean out the window to yell at the guy some more. She is leaning over me and I slowly start going deaf from the cursing and screaming going into my right ear. The scene continues as we drive down Paisano street and ends only when my grandmother sits back down in the middle of the seat and starts combing her disheveled hair. She looks over at me and says,

"*Mijo, quieres que te compre una nieve*?" as if nothing had occurred.

"*Si*, lets go get some ice cream, *vamos Leo a comprarles a los niños una nieve,*" she says to my father who is turning red in the face and is mumbling something under his breath about a "*vieja loca.*"

My mother clutches her heart and looks at my grandma while she says something about driving her crazy. She then tends to my little brother who has a heel mark firmly implanted on his forehead. I smile at my grandmother who hugs me hard and we both laugh in the back seat as we drive down to buy some ice creams down at the bodega.

# CHAPTER SEVEN

The mid seventies was a period of great change for me. I met a good woman and although still relatively young, decided to snap her up and try to start a new life with her before someone else did. I had made it very clear to her though that if we were to have any type of future together, she would have to meet the matriarch of the family, my grandmother, and have to pass approval. If she didn't then any future together was not meant to be.

My grandmother had been a major influence up to this point in my life, more so than anyone else. I was entering young adulthood and the plan was to finish school, marry a good woman and leave for the military where I could get a leg up on some sort of life.

This period of my life was around ten years after the passage of the great civil rights bill of the sixties. People's attitudes however do not change with a stroke of a pen. The process of equality in this society is a much slower train and at times ignores progress by ignoring designated stops along the way. Life is not always lived as it is intended to be. I figured a couple of years in the military would at least give me an opportunity for some sort of a start somewhere. At this point in life, I was leaving the era of my youth and coming into my own as an adult so I took stock of the people around me who had influenced me and who had been with me for so long.

My mother was a deliberate woman who had not known much happiness in her life. She was the first-born to my grandmother and Mexican tradition called for her to play the role of semi-mother to all her siblings. If at any time, upon the death or the loss of her mother's spouse, she as the oldest was required to provide care and comfort for her mother until such time as she decided to remarry or until her death. To me, this always sounded like a contract between the oldest daughter and the mother and it appeared to me that the only thing lacking was a signed document between the two.

My mother believed in this tradition and followed it to its fullest. When she turned sixteen she became infatuated with a man four years her senior. In those days, people lived in a form of *ejido* housing which is similar to tenement housing or duplexes that share a common courtyard. Homes would be clustered together along dirt roads and usually one family branched out and lived side by side in small three or four house tracts. Each family lived in small homes not much bigger than shacks where daily duties were shared. The cooking might be done solely in one home while the washing would be done in another. This was the old Mexican form of communal living and a residence was designated more by a landmark instead of a street address.

My grandmother told me that when they left railroad work and settled in El Paso, she'd give directions to her home as being three blocks down from the paved street until you came to the old elm tree, turn left and walk about a half a mile down past the canal onto the caliche road where you could see the house.

My mother was required to help with chores and keep her brothers and sisters in line. She was a young and impressionable sixteen-year-old girl who became smitten with one of the worst kind. She fell in love with a Mejicano transplant from the old country who still believed in the old ways of the old country where women were considered nothing more than conquests for men. Since my original grandfather was a dominating and cruel hearted bastard (my grandmothers own words, not mine) who did not possess the ability to show affection for his children and who imbedded discipline into his children by way of the whip, my mother sought refuge from this life and easily fell into a web of love and lies initiated by this young, handsome Mejicano.

She fell in love and allowed her youthful intuition to get the better of her. Relying on the promise of the young man to marry her and believing everything would turn out all right, she reluctantly had to tell her parents she was pregnant. The young and precocious girl was bitterly disappointed when she found out she was just another notch on his list of conquests.

My real grandfather had threatened to send my mother away to a convent in Mexico where she would be forced to deliver the baby and live the life of a nun while the child was placed up for adoption. Here she would be banished to a life of servitude as her penance. But my grandmother had stood up for her oldest daughter and argued against this. This was the scenario that triggered the decision by my grandmother to leave my original grandfather.

There had been many fights between the two, some had been ugly and all had been loud. This fight exhibited the stubbornness of both, each clinging to a belief that they knew what was best for the child. After a day or two of shouting and screaming at each other, my grandmother packed up all of my grandfather's belongings and with the help of her brothers still living in El Paso, forced, or rather convinced, my grandfather to leave the house. This left my grandmother with five children and one grandchild on the way to raise by herself.

The departure of her husband allowed for the termination of a violent and turbulent marriage for my grandmother. On the other hand it only strengthened my grandmother's will to succeed on her own. This only brought mother and daughter closer to each other since this is where the chain of events began that strengthened their bond.

I never did find out who my older brother's father was. My grandmother would only refer to him as "*aquel pinche*" and so I naturally assumed that his first name was *aquel* and his last name was *pinche.* It was only after much later when I started using profanity that I came to understand this was not his real name.

I do remember one day as a child when my mother took me on a trip to downtown El Paso. I must not have been older than nine or ten and we were walking down the street when a man approached my mother and stopped us in front of the old Popular Department Store. My mother was in her mid to late thirties and I saw the expression on her face freeze in a type of shocked and angry look. The man clearly in his forties and dressed in what was then referred to as a "jiddy" look, (which was someone trying to look younger and hipper than his age) stood in front of us. He had a sort of smirk on his face. I first noticed him standing outside a bar talking to a woman who looked like a cheap prostitute and he called out my mother's name as we passed by.

Being nine years old, I couldn't understand the conversation between them. I do remember looking at her face and seeing it turn from white to red with a look of surprise and anger. I didn't like this man and I made sure I gave him a look that said as much. I remember he looked down and touched me on the head to rub it in a sort of condescending manner. I pulled my head away and he laughed. My mother responded to him in a bitter manner and told him not to touch me. As we walked away, she brushed right by him as if to show she had gotten the better end of the deal from the relationship.

Although she tried hard not to show it, she was visibly shaken and I remember when we got on the bus to go home, she started to cry into her Kleenex. This concerned me as it would any nine year old when he sees their mother crying and has no idea what's going on. I asked her what was wrong. "*Nada mijo*" she said, "*no es nada.*" She wept quietly as she stared out the window while the bus rolled along back to my grandma's house. I remember I wrapped my arms around her as tight as I could hoping I could make whatever pain she was feeling go away. She held me in her arms as she leaned her head on the window and relieved the pain of a love lost long ago.

When we arrived at my grandmother's house, I heard them talking and my mother told her about the encounter with the man on the street. I knew this was my half brother's father since my grandmother kept referring to him as *aquel pinche*..

Because of this incident in my mothers young life and because of the issue involving my grandmother's divorce, a strong and sturdy bond held together both mother and daughter. When David was born, my grandmother helped raise him while my mother worked.

In her twenties, my mother worked at a Woolworth's store when they still ran those soda fountain/diner operations. She worked there for many years and along with the cooking expertise passed on to her from my grandmother, she became a very good cook. To this day I can still say I have never eaten a sandwich as good as those prepared by my mother.

When she was young, she drank and smoked like my grandmother but by the time she met my father, she quit drinking and never touched another drop for the rest of her life. She was a humble woman who worked hard and for some reason I always thought she felt as though her one chance at love had come and gone. I sensed from her a sort of resigned acceptance as to how her life turned out.

I perceived her to be a person who once allowed herself the pleasure of breaking away from the safe confines of her life to take a gamble on love and loss. She lived her life as a dedicated daughter who cared for her mother first and foremost. She took pride in her children and of course, we as her children occupied a special place in her heart. I always thought she felt scared to allow her life to once again feel or express any joy. It was as if she swam out to the deep end of a pool when told not to and for that, she had almost drowned. Now, back in the safety of her common life, she was not about to take any more chances.

This was her true calling in life and she was content to live it with no more surprises. As I grew older in life, I went from a feeling of confusion about this to a feeling of sorrow. I was confused at her lack of motivation to experience so many things in life, to live it to its fullest and to learn from its mistakes and its triumphs. When I learned the stories told to me by my grandmother and my aunts and uncles and those who knew of her life, I realized how she had once been a rambunctious person eager to get away from a hard life and experience joy only to be met by heartbreak. Upon returning to her life, her parents separated due to an incident of her own doing. Not the sole reason of course but a last straw in an already doomed marriage. As much as I loved my grandmother then, now, and always, I know she was also instrumental in keeping a sense of guilt attached to my mother's conscience.

In her twenties when she met my father, my mother was very straightforward with regards to how things would be with her mother. She would still be at her beckon call to provide anything she needed and if he had a problem with that, better to speak now or not even bother. She came with a package deal and caring for her mother was an integral part of that plan. My father agreed and accepted this condition. When the time came for my mother to leave my grandmother's house, there was a decision to be made and again, it was one based on tales from the old country. Since both mother and grandmother had raised my half brother together, it was only natural he developed an attachment to my grandmother. Leaving the only home he'd known would prove difficult. The basis for the argument to remain with my grandmother arose from a story later told to me by my Aunt Josefina many years later.

It seems that early on in my grandmother's life, before she had my mother, there had been another child born, a first-born son. The child had been born while grandma still worked on the rail lines. Her older sister Tencha had hired a local woman to care for the child while everyone worked and the woman would be responsible solely for the care of the child. The old woman was from Mexico, recommended by a friend of a friend. In those days, word of mouth was the only form of reference.

The woman cared for the child and when the infant was six months old, the time came to move on to the next town and lay the next section of track. The old Mexican woman resisted the effort to move with my grandmother's family since she was too old and because she wanted no part of their nomad lifestyle. My grandmother thought the woman to be crazy and told her if she could not fulfill the duties she was hired for, then there was no need for her services anymore and she should return to Mexico. The old woman, who had become attached to the child, told my grandmother she could not take the baby from her care. The old woman became enraged and told her that if she took the child, a spell would be placed on the child and he would die. My grandmother being the fearless woman she was, cast aside the warning and told the old woman she was crazy. The old woman told my grandmother that from now on, each first born child would suffer the same fate. So they may know the pain caused by taking away this child from her.

The family group left the old woman at camp and departed with the railroad crews the next day. Two days later, the infant developed a cough. Three days later, the child was dead. My grandmother was heartbroken. She blamed herself for not believing the old woman. She was angry with herself and carried the burden of the old woman's curse for many years. Perhaps it was a coincidence that the child died at that time. There were many variables to consider and medicine then was not what it is today. Maybe the spell was true, we will never know. Personally, I never believed it to be true but apparently people didn't know any better in those days so the story only gave my grandmother more ammunition when talking my mother into letting her keep David to raise herself.

It became rather evident that when my mother was ready to start her life with my father there was a reluctance on the part of my grandmother to allow both of them to leave. The night before their wedding, the last night my mother spent as a single woman, her mother came and told her the story of her firstborn and the old woman. How my mother had originally had an older brother and how he had died as predicted. My mother, fearing that the same fate would befall her child, agreed to leave David to be raised by my grandmother. Unknown to her at the time, she helped create an irreversible mistake that even to this day still leaves repercussions. My brother David, while raised by my grandmother, never did reach his full potential. My grandmother tried to make up for all the times she had worked. The times which had not allowed her the opportunity to enjoy motherhood. She spoiled him blind. My aunts and uncles were all grown now and David presented her with an opportunity to do it all over again. Although my father had agreed to and was willing to raise the child as his own, he never stood between the decision made between mother and daughter and stood by in silence as my half brother lived a life without discipline.

My grandmother spoiled him and without the presence of any discipline, he never did amount to much. He lived on the streets and ran with the wrong crowds. When he was fourteen, he was picked up for auto theft. When he was sixteen he was kicked out of school. At seventeen he got a shy fifteen-year-old girl named Blanca pregnant. The only good thing about this was that eventually she would become my sister in law and someone whom I adored very much. She bore him five sons and even to this day, is still legally married to him though they only lived together as man and wife for around five years. He was in and out of prison. His whole adult life was spent committing one crime after another. In his fifty-six years alive, forty have been spent behind bars.

The one thing he was good at was that he yearned to please my grandmother. When he disobeyed her, she would whip him with a piece of garden hose when he was bad. He would clean up his act for a while but eventually he would revert to his old self and run the streets with the barrio boys, break into homes, get caught and get sent back to prison. This broke my mother's heart and I believe that before she died, she knew that leaving him with my grandmother had been a mistake.

This issue also became a factor in my relationship with my grandmother. I always felt my mother was uncomfortable with me being so close to her. She never said it but I always felt as if my mother didn't think we should be so close. I guess she felt she didn't want to lose another one. This always made for an uncomfortable relation between the three of us and I was never able to truly understand why.

My father watched David grow and waste his life. Although they got along, he always regretted not having stood up to my grandmother and taken the boy while he was still young. Although my mother served as the dutiful daughter, there was always this unspoken issue lying just beneath the surface as to whose fault it was that he turned out the way he did. My half brother would write my grandmother from prison and she in turn would tell my mother how he was doing. He never wrote to my mother until years later. When I found out, this bothered me greatly. Then I found out he had not even been told that my mother was also his mother. At a very young age, he was told that my mother was his older sister and not until he was sent to prison in his late twenties was he told that she was not a sister but his biological mother.

He and I shared very few times together since the age difference between us was a major factor. But I just treated him as another family member. I didn't really think about him until we embarked on the infamous Alameda bar trips of my childhood.

# CHAPTER EIGHT

One thing David had applied himself to and learned very well was how to play guitar. My grandmother loved to sing and party and in his quest to satisfy her he learned to play excellent guitar. There was no doubt this type of activity was where he learned to party and quench his taste for music. When he was young, my grandmother encouraged him to learn to play. He did so with a dedicated fervor that while in his teens, he became a great player of traditional *ranchera* and *corrida* music. Mexican *Norteno* music was born in the bars of the old country and transplanted to the barrios of El Paso and other border towns. They were made for those long lonely nights at a bar when a man goes to drown his sorrows and get over the painful breakup of a lost love. Norteño music is the theme song to this emotion and David learned to play with the best of them.

At seventeen and expecting a baby with my sister in law Blanca, money was a sought after commodity. One quick way of making fast money was to play music at the bars that lined the streets of Alameda Boulevard in El Paso. In those days, Alameda Street was full of life and it was a vibrant place to experience the *Bolero* and *Norteno* sounds of Juarez and other parts of old Mexico. It was the heart of Mejicano town in El Paso and every city along the border had a street like it. A night out on the town meant visiting the bars and restaurants, some seedy but most evoking the style of a nice place to have some drinks and listen to good music. It was a piece of the past in the present and anyone with the talent to bring the music to life came to be well known and respected.

Into this world entered my half brother David with his ability to memorize songs, play guitar and sing the songs of the heart, of suffering and tears and all that love entails. He was truly good and his gift was his ability to make money at it. It also gave him a sense of pride knowing people respected his ability, something he had never experienced before. He teamed up with two other friends who also played guitar and between the three of them they followed the tradition of "*los trios*" that went from bar to bar to playing songs for money. People paid to hear good music and this created a market of competing trios, each trying to outdo the other by matching their talents against one another. Many times, one would compete against the other, leaving it to the bar crowd to determine who was the best.

My brother David and his crew never lost. Losers were obligated to buy beers for the winners. This made for frequent fights at my grandmother's house when David showed up late at night drunk from a night of singing and carousing with women. There were always women. My grandmother would again be babysitting us and would yell and tell him to grow up and be more responsible "*Tienes una familia y tienes que ser responsible,*" she would yell. He would stagger over to her and always begin to serenade her with a favorite song, at which point a smile would come over her face and she would join him in singing. By the third song, my grandma Lencha would have a drink and a smoke in her hand and once again, David knew he had gotten away with it.

One day my grandma Lencha came up with an idea. "*Mira* David, I am getting tired of you going out so much and coming home drunk three or four nights a week," she said. "You have to get up for work the next day and you don't get up on time. Mijo you have been late to work at the plant twice last week and they have warned you about losing your job," she pleaded. "I don't want you to drink so much when you go out and play so starting tomorrow, this is what you are going to do."

I was sitting with my little brother watching the wrestling matches on TV. On the screen, the Mexican wrestler El SANTO was standing in the middle of the ring holding another wrestler over his head like an airplane. He was getting ready to do a knee slam on the guy and the referee was trying to get him to let go. EL SANTO was a famous masked wrestler from Mexico who never took his mask off. In English it stands for the saint and when he wrestled, he always played the part of the good guy. Nobody ever knew his real identity. Kind of like a Spanish version of Superman and he even appeared in comic books and in movies. EL SANTO was cool. I was waiting for El Santo to apply the death drop to the evil wrestler and make everything good in the world when just then my grandmother grabbed me by the arm and pulled me up and stood me in front of David who was in a drunken stupor trying his best to remain standing up while tuning his guitar.

"*Mira*" says my grandmother "*manana, te llevas al niño contigo cuando vayan a tocar música*," she held me up and pointed to me as if I were some type of carpet sample she was showing to a customer.

"*Ama, pero como,*" yelled David. He never called her grandma and none of us ever dared call her Lencha. It was either "granma" or "Ama." "How am I supposed to take care of this *mocosio* and play musica? This is my work. I go and make money. I don't have time to baby-sit him," he pointed at me.

I really didn't care or knew what was going on since I was trying to turn to see the wrestling match on TV. EL SANTO was cool!

"*Yo no se, pero te lo vas a llevar*," said my grandmother and that was that. She had the look on her face that said, "That's it" end of argument.

Even in his stupor, David glared at me since he knew this was the end of the argument and had lost. As best as I could figure, I was supposed to go with him and do something although I didn't know what. So the next day, around five I was sitting outside throwing the football around with my little brother when David called me from the house. The football, of course, was from Sears.

"*Ven aqui cabron,.*" Since most of the adults called me *cabron* and I was still too young to know any better, I always responded when someone yelled *cabron* in my general direction. I was young and I figured it might be some type of term of endearment. I figured everyone called me that because they cared, Boy was I stupid or what.

Anyway, when I got to the door, David was telling me to get inside and clean myself up "*Andale cabron, y límpiate esos pinche oídos.*" I don't know how he could tell my ears were dirty. They were caked with dirt from rolling around in the brown dirt outside playing with my football from Sears but I didn't think they were dirty.

Ten minutes later I find myself in the car that Rica is driving. Rica is David's best friend who also plays guitar and we're on the way to pick up Beto, the third guy in the trio. As I then came to find out, my grandmother's intent was to have David take me along when he went out and play with his "trio." In her way of thinking, if you drag along a ten-year-old kid, you can't get into too much trouble towing him around. How could you drink that much taking care of a ten- year-old? If anything happened to me, David was going to get it.

Trouble was, I knew my brother David didn't want to take me along and frankly I didn't want to come along. My grandmother insisted and he and I both knew that this was to be done because grandma Lencha said so. I was the collar around his neck. At first, he took it out on me but he knew if anything happened, there would be hell to pay.

This was a very enlightening experience in my life. Up to now, my thoughts had been preoccupied by playing in the dirt, toy soldiers from Sears and watching EL SANTO on TV. When we got to the first bar, David knew the owner and all the bartenders. He had been performing in "trios" for almost a year now and everyone knew him and marveled at his talent. This included, of course, women. The women who worked at these bars were very well endowed, waiting on tables and serving the liquor. Sometimes they were waitresses and sometimes they worked behind the bar.

This was the sixties and the fashion of the day was a tight dress. The Sophia Loren look which revealed a lot of cleavage. In Mexico, women like Maria Felix and Lola Beltran copied this Hollywood fashion statement that displayed the provocative but well-heeled womanly look. Naturally, this filtered down to the bars and nightclubs around the country and El Paso was no different. Even the old magazines of the time with their pictures of white gringas mirrored the look although I had never really seen any gringas in person.

David would take me into a bar holding my hand and would have to go explain to the owner that I was with him. Since everyone knew that David's "trio" was good and since music was good for business no one objected. So I was told to sit down at the far end of the bar and I was given a coca-cola with ice and told by David to shut up and sit quietly.

"*Sientate hay cabron y callate lo sico,*" He called me a cabron so he must love me, right?. I would do as I was told and sit at the far end of the bar not bothering anybody. Immediately the waitresses or the bartender, if she was a female, would come over to where I was sitting. I was not quite tall enough to sit and look over the bar from my stool so inevitably I was told to sit up or I was picked up by someone and placed on the bar counter. This always happened and the women would either pinch my cheek or tussle my hair. But this was not what kept my attention. My first impression of women's breasts was one of curiosity and confusion.

I got to see all kinds of breasts. Large and small-breasted women would come over to me and say, "*mira que chulo cabroncito.*" Again, I thought this was a term of endearment and coming from large breasted women, well she could have pretty much called me whatever she wanted. They would say this as I stared at their large bosoms while they patted me on the head or they squeezed my cheeks. They didn't mind me staring at them and they would make silly comments about it but I didn't care. Hell, they could have called me *pinche desgraciado* for all I cared. Some of them would cuddle me and hold me to their chests. I could smell the cheap perfume and would snuggle my face into their enormous breasts. I thought I was in heaven. Others would want to play with me and ask me what my name was, how old I was, things like that. But after a couple of times I started acting dumb and would pretend to get my age wrong by displaying two hands with eight fingers up, then nine, then eight and so on. For some reason, they thought this was the cutest thing. They thought a kid who was trying real hard to show whether he was eight, or nine or ten looked sooo cute trying to figure it out.

"*Mira, que chulo,*" they'd say and squeeze me into their breasts again and hug me tight and I couldn't breathe into their chests. I would try real hard again and they would hug me again and… this would go on for about ten minutes until the men in the bar would start making smart comments like, "*Dejalo resollar*" and "*Lo vas a ahogar.*"

Sometimes everyone would laugh out loud and say something funny which made the women hug me some more. I would get another coke and …aahh, life was good back then! After this, I had a fine appreciation for a woman's body and suddenly toy soldiers didn't seem quite as important to me as they used to be. I think I got a head start on puberty, which was fine by me. I only went with David for a couple of weeks since after awhile when it came time to leave after his set, he would yell at me from the door to catch up because he was leaving.

"*Andale cabron, vamonos,*" he would say. As the night would grow longer, he would become more and more agitated and yell at me in a harsher tone. By the last few bars of the night, I had to keep an eye on him since a couple of times, he even forgot to call out to me. I was afraid he would leave me behind.

He was still getting drunk. My presence did nothing to slow down his intoxicating habits. Then reluctantly, my grandmother thought the safest thing to do was to keep me from going with him because she was afraid we might all get killed in some traffic accident so I didn't get to go anymore. What a shame.

The last night she sent me with him, David did leave me at the "Tres Aces" bar. I was playing behind the counter trying to get quarters out of the spaces along the bar sidings where customers sometimes dropped their change. I had small hands so I could easily reach in and pull the loose change out, this one particular night I finished and got up to look for David. I looked and looked but he was gone. Some other trio was playing music and he was nowhere around. I didn't care. Filiberto was the owner of the bar and he was kind to me so I wasn't worried. Besides, once my grandmother found out, I was not going to be the one in trouble, he was.

I sat at the end of the bar and waited until the man I remember as my second grandfather Fidel came into the bar. By this time, my grandma and he had gotten married and this was during the early part of the marriage when he was still a nice guy trying to make points with all the family members.

David had called home and told Fidel that they were playing at some bar and that they were too busy to go back and pick me up and could he go get me. An invite to a bar was something Fidel would not pass up so he had come down with my tio Manuel and they let me play a while longer while they both had a beer and talked to Filiberto the owner.

After that, David tended to avoid me and didn't go out and do much guitar playing. He was too tied up with Blanca and the pending arrival of the new baby. He no longer had time to go play with his trio much less talk to me. About a month later, he got picked up for theft of auto. He went away for a couple of years and missed the birth of his first born son, whom my sister in law Blanca named, David Jr.

# CHAPTER NINE

My father was more of an introvert, someone without the ability to openly express emotion. The only times he did was when he was under the warm induced spell of alcohol. He was not a cruel man as per se but he was someone who did not possess the ability to express his emotions toward others. When something bothered him, he would drink and allow his state of inebriation to bring relief from what ailed him. Still, he kept it all inside. In the early years, he drank a lot. Much later in my life, I came to find out that his mother was from a well to do ranching family in Chihuahua. She had defied her fathers wishes and married a commoner who had worked on the farm at one time during her early teens, this being my paternal grandfather.

Her family had disavowed her and she was banished from the family when she married a good yet poor man who loved her very much. They both left Chihuahua bound for the United States during the revolutionary years in Mexico and settled in Juarez. Both waited for the opportunity to cross the river and find something secure in the United States. In those days, there were many refugees in Ciudad Juarez due to the revolution in Mexico. The war dragged on and then as now, the United States tried hard to stem the flow coming across its southern border. At the time, a written guarantee of work in El Paso from an American employer would expedite the journey into this country. Those were few and hard to come by. His mother had no relatives that could help. His father had two sisters and his mother who lived in Juarez but all in the same boat. All desperate to get out of the country and try their luck in the U.S.

His father had a distant cousin living in El Paso who had promised to try and get them across via his contacts at a textile factory in El Paso where he worked. At the time, these were run by segments of large Chinese immigrants that had settled there and understood the difficulties of escaping the hardships of their homelands.

My father had a brother, my uncle Manny who was the first-born in the family. They were the only two children born of this marriage. The reason was that my paternal grandmother had died while giving birth to my father. The family secret, as far as I could tell, was that my father's father had never forgiven my father for her death and had never really gotten over her death.

Many said that my grandfather was so heartbroken that he left my father with his sister, my fathers aunt who raised him until he was thirteen years of age. He had left his brother, my uncle Manny in the care of his mother. My grandfather had then traveled the United States in search of work far away from El Paso and far from the memory of his beloved wife.

He found a job in Wyoming working on cattle ranches and he would send money home to his sisters and his mother to help in raising the two boys. When my father turned thirteen, his father came back from Wyoming to fetch him and take him back to work at the ranch up north. No one really quite knows what happened during this time period. This is one of those times that no one ever knew what happened since he never talked about it.

When I became older into my twenties I tried to establish some type of bond between my father and myself. I can only recall having a beer with him not more than twice in my entire life. A couple of times I tried to bring up the story to verify any facts I had heard but it was all to no avail. He never spoke of those times in Wyoming. I can remember he admitted to me only twice that he had even been there. Yes, he had gone with his father but that was the extent of what he would admit to.

My father and his brother Manny were not very close at all. Matter of fact, I was in my thirties when I found out that he and his family lived only eight miles from where we had grown up. They lived in the middle class neighborhood known as Lakeside but the two brothers had not seen or spoken to each other in the last fifteen years. Neither ever attempted to make contact with the other and the only contact ever made between both families had been by chance.

When my mother herself turned fifty, she pursued something she had always wanted to accomplish. She had never learned to drive and on her fiftieth birthday, she expressed an interest in taking driving lessons at the nearby college. As it just so happened, my tia Susana who married my father's brother had also signed up for the same driving class. The two women had not seen each other for years since apparently there had been a falling out. No one would ever say what it had been about. Still, my father was not the type of person who would pick up a phone to be sociable, even with his own brother.

In my thirties, I tried reaching out to my tio Manny to find out more about my father's life. My tio Manny verified a lot of what had been rumors. Apparently, during the trip to Wyoming between father and son, things had been hashed out between both of them. My grandfather had expressed his grief and sorrow and had blamed my father as the reason for the loss of his wife. My father had not taken this criticism well and had withdrawn into his own emotional shell.

In his life he had endured the loss of his mother who had died while giving birth to him. Now he was made to feel guilty about it, when actually, he had never had any fault in the matter to begin with. At the age of thirteen he was removed from the only home he had known, to travel with a man who claimed to be his father but who was in truth a stranger to him. They had returned to El Paso when he was about to turn seventeen and my mother once told me that he had told her once that he had felt very alienated during those years up north. He had come back a changed man. He had only been around women who cared for him and raised him in El Paso and Ciudad. Juarez. In Wyoming, he lived with wranglers and cowboys who watched out for themselves. These cowboys did not understand family life and were devoid of emotions. Everyday, life revolved around hard work. On weekends they would blow off steam with the no name whores and bartenders in the nearby town.

When he came back he had not yet met my mother. His aunt had married a Mejicano who was born in El Paso and they had moved across the border to live in the United States. Upon his return from Wyoming he lived with her for a while. This was 1941 before the start of the war and without the knowledge of the pending events about to change the course of history. Not finding any worthwhile opportunity in El Paso, he enlisted in the U.S. Army and was shipped overseas the following year. He was wounded at the Battle of the Bulge during the war and received the Purple Heart and a silver star for bravery. Again I never knew nor did he ever tell us the story of his gallantry when we asked him about these medals. When he returned to El Paso he got a job as a taxi driver. That was when he met my mother.

He never lost his sense of demeanor. His character flaw was that he was very good at holding things in, never wishing to share anything with anyone. My mother was pretty much the only person he would talk to and even then, in her later years she once told me that my father never liked to talk much about himself or the past. This was OK with her since she was always too busy with my grandma Lencha or she was raising us. This didn't leave too much time for too much else. I always perceived theirs to be a marriage of convenience and although it makes me feel wrong to say this, I truly did believe this. Perhaps my siblings may disagree on this point but growing up, I felt as if each lived their life in their own world. I do believe there was a love between them. They remained married to each other their entire lives and there had to have been some emotional attachment between the two. But I never thought it reflected what I came to understand a marriage was supposed to be. I suppose in those days as now, people have their own reason for taking the leap of marriage. One man's logic may be another man's fear. Yet at times, I thought we all had our doubts as to whether they would last but they did. My perception of their marriage was one of a partnership but not of a true love romance. For better or for worse, this was the arrangement that fit their lives. My perception of my father was that of the man who went away during the day to make money to support us.

As far as any bonding with me, his first-born son it was probably the same for me as it had been for him. Apart from sitting down and listening to him rattle on in a drunken stupor, repeating the same stories, hearing the same complaints against the neighbor, the government and watching him nod off after finally feeling the effects of the liquor, that was all there was to our relationship. He never talked about the war. He never talked about his childhood. As far back as I can recall, he never really opened up too much. The liquor brought him solace and comfort and provided an escape from the reality of life.

In the early years of my parents' marriage, my oldest sister told me about his violent temper and how he could explode with rage at the smallest of things. Once, he threw a telephone at her when she came home late from school and put a gash over her eye that required five stitches. When he was hungover, we always knew we were to keep quiet and stay out of his way. The television was to be kept low. If you acted up or got loud, boy you really paid for it. This led to many loud fights between my mother and father that were pretty nasty. I can recall many times my mother would gather us up and pack our clothes and we would have to walk to my grandmother's house. Because of some serious fights, my mother would take us away and leave him for a few days. Eventually he would come over to my grandmother's house and we would go back home. I was never really close to my father and his refusal to open up and connect cost our relationship dearly.

During the time I was between thirteen and seventeen years of age, we did not speak to each other. There had been some stupid fight between us that ended up with him throwing me out of the house. My mother brought me back in and we just never spoke, about the fight, or about regrets or anything. Nothing. I cannot recall any one time when we had a discussion with any substance. When he went to Phoenix to fetch me I knew at least what to expect. I felt he was at least paying attention to me. The others wondered how bad it would be with their father. I knew how bad it would be with mine. Perhaps that's what our relationship was about. I knew him only too well, but not at all.

The only time I approached him to ask him anything was when he was having his beers, that period right after the second beer and before inebriation takes over. His feelings of regret on not raising David had been told to me during one of those times. He would sit outside in his kitchen chair on the small cement slab that passed for a porch at our home. I would try and pick out the issues of substance on anything that gave a hint as to what he was thinking. After a while, I just got tired and didn't want to try anymore. He never spoke of his past, his family, childhood, or anything that involved him. When he died, I felt he had died a very lonely man, occupying space but not really here. Probably glad that it was all over with. When we buried him, I wished him eternal peace.

# CHAPTER TEN

"You cannot leave me mijo because I am afraid that you won't come back!" The tears welled up in my grandmother's big dark eyes as she looked at me and tried hard to convince me into staying.

I had just turned nineteen years old and I wanted to avoid being drafted into the army. So I figured I would beat Uncle Sam to the punch and enlist in the Navy. I always yearned to go see the world. Recently married, it would give me an opportunity to start my life off on some type of positive step. The government had introduced the GI Bill as a way to reward those who volunteered to serve their country. I figured I'd do my three years and come back to enroll at the University and pursue an academic degree while getting paid for it. It was a step up from the low paying jobs and dim career prospects of El Paso at the time. I had a child on the way and I refused to allow myself to continue in the cycle of poverty I had known all my life.

We weren't dirt poor, thankfully we had food on the table and a roof over our heads. Compared to others we were one step above poor and two steps below middle class. I look back and understand that my father did the best he could in raising three girls and two boys. I wanted to break out of this dreary low wage existence and take my chances at something better, albeit not having a clue as to what.

Still, military service was a way out of the doldrums. So I chose what I felt was the best opportunity to succeed. My mother, although having understood my reasoning, remained quiet on the matter. She never really discouraged me from going, yet I knew she didn't want me to go. My Tia Aurora and Tia Josefina's sons Johnny and Ruben, had gone to Vietnam. They had come back different in their way of thinking to say the least. They viewed the world through a different prism now. They had passed through the portal of life from family youngsters to men who had seen the ugliness of war.

Two cousins from my Tio Francisco's clan had been killed in action. They were awarded the Purple Heart and Silver Star for bravery. They continued in the tradition of Mexican American soldiers who volunteered to fight defending this country. They had gambled on a future but had come home in a box.

My Tio Francisco was crushed. Since my grandma and he were close, she felt his pain and understood his loss. It was something she was not anxious to experience in her life just yet, especially with me. My mother was afraid of losing her first-born son. She understood though that I was making my sojourn into manhood. I was trying to become a responsible person and that meant a tear in the emotional tie between mother and son. She would worry about me on her own, silently, always praying, trying to come to grips with raising a son born into the violent world of the barrios of south El Paso. She understood that my time had come to move on. She understood I was not hers to care for anymore.

Now she was faced with the possibility of me either surviving this episode or losing me in some strange war she didn't understand. She knew I could get killed on the other side of the world. Though the war in Vietnam was winding down, it was still a war and people were still dying. She was proud but worried for me as only a mother can. I knew there would be many candles lit at the San Juan Catholic Church and many hours spent praying for a safe return home.

She had made me promise to go and tell my grandmother of my impending departure. I dreaded this duty. I knew I would carry it out as a devoted son. I also knew that my grandmother had recently gotten the news that her brother Francisco's son had been killed in action. The timing of my decision to enlist was not good. I was not aware that his death was the result of the fighting overseas, that the cold hands of the grim reaper were now hitting so close to home.

Every week, a family in the barrio somewhere was losing a son or at times a daughter to the fighting overseas. I often wondered about this and wondered why my family would be any different in avoiding this fate? The timing was just bad. This made my inevitable trip to my grandmother's house even more depressing. I knew I would need to show her the strength she had instilled in me. Now more than ever, my ability to control my fears and exhibit the strength of her strength was to be tested. I was like her in so many ways. Someday I would need to show her I had become as strong as she had come to expect. What I did not expect was that the first test of this strength would have to be in facing off against her.

A test of wills between a third person and myself was understandable. A test against her will was not. I knew the road that lay ahead of me. The Saturday before departing to boot camp in California, I stood before her, gripped my teeth and saw the tears start to flow down her cheek. I tried to say something in a calming voice to reinforce the nature that everything would be all right.

As I opened my mouth to form the words, no sound came out. I felt a rush of emotion come over me. I decided to close my mouth before the onset of emotions would cause me to choke on my own words. My emotions had betrayed me. A rush of sobs was close to erupting from my own tortured soul since I never liked to see her hurt. Yet here I was responsible for making her feel that which I had always defended her against. I went to sit down next to her and let her know that everything would be OK. I did not want her to cry because she was my grandma. I loved her so much that I felt her pain.

I knew I could not do that. I gritted my teeth and clenched my fist while I took periodical looks up to the ceiling of the little house to prevent tears from flowing freely down my cheeks. It is a moment when one wonders how much of an emotional toll the human body can endure. How it aligns itself by a true moment of resistance we call strength. It is a choice between doing what you wish to do and what you need to do. What is said versus what you wish to say. It was not an easy moment. I stood there in front of her unable to use my voice. My body is stiff from straining every muscle to keep from dropping to my knees, telling her I would not go. I wanted to tell her I changed my mind. I would not leave her to go off and die.

At that moment I understood everything I had come to know about this woman from her past. I understood what she must have gone through as a child raised during the depression, to have been born on the wrong side of the gringo line. Having to escape the violence in order to survive. To be chastised by others for it and go straight to an adult life with no requiem of any childhood. To understand that in life, misery and happiness travel hand in hand down the same path.

Deep down inside my soul I gathered a strength I had not known, a strength that would hereafter be there as a result of this encounter. I looked her straight in the eye and said, " I'm going to be fine, I don't want you to worry about me because I'm going to be back before you know it." I struggled to put a smile on my face.

"Who else will be here to listen to your stories and light your cigarettes for you and fetch your whiskey?" I joked. I bit my tongue and forced an even bigger smile and I could see the tip of her lips start an upward curve to configure a smile. She gulped down her tears and wiped away at another, which rolled down her cheek to the tip of her chin.

"You are right mijo, who else but you can have the patience to put up with this old *vieja* and all my bad habits. *Dios quiera*, you will be home very soon and I will have my *cabroncito* back with me".

I smiled in agreement and felt the knots in my stomach start to ease up but still keep a good vise grip on my insides. I steadied myself and sat down next to her and put my hand over hers. "Don't worry so much about me, you need to take care of yourself," I said. She put her other hand on my cheek and looked into my eyes with a longing I had not seen since I was a small boy.

"You have grown up so big and so fast. I remember just yesterday you would fall asleep by my side on that warm sweater of mine that you liked so much. And look at you now, all grown up going off to war".

When saying this, her smile turned into a frown. She gripped my chin and raised it up until her eyes were even with mine. She slapped me, not too hard, but hard enough to get my attention, "*Mira cabron, vale mas que te cuides allá y no hagas cualquier pendejada para que te maten aquellos hijos de la shingada*!"

Her finger was pointed exactly at my nose and she kept wiggling it back and forth, scolding me to make her point. I better not do anything stupid and get myself killed or there would be hell to pay. I don't know what scared me more, the fact that I could possibly be killed or that if I died she would bring me back to life to kill me again. Now there's a thought!

"*Si* grandma, don't worry I'll take care of myself. I'll be back," I said as I kissed her on the cheek.

I knew her thoughts were on my cousin Gregorio and what had been his fate. He was a good guy. I remember him always having a sense of humor. Quick with a joke, he always infected everyone around him with his laughter. He was one of my Tio Francisco's favorite grandkids. What he lacked in height, he made up for with strength. A strong bulky character of 5'10", he had played high school football in Los Angeles and made all conference his senior year. I heard he had joined the Marines on a four-year tour. He was sent to Vietnam someplace in the middle of the country. He almost made it out alive with one year to go before his tour was up. I heard he planned on coming home and continuing his studies to get a jump start on something, just like me.

For so many Hispanics, those of us who did not or could not take advantage of a continuing education, the military was a way out of the barrios. When I went in, I saw so much *Raza* I couldn't believe there were that many of us out there. We were all trying to find the magical key to open up a door to our future.

Since I was also my mother's son, she too would miss me. The woman who brought me into this world was willing to let me go then so must my grandmother. The underlying connection between mother and daughter with me in the middle had come to a fork in the road. The path taken was chosen by me though begrudgingly accepted by both. I would leave concerned with the impact it would have on both of them and wondered if they would be different upon my return.

I applied all the reasoning that a nineteen-year-old with little experience along with the arrogance of youth could muster. I convinced myself that things would never change. That somehow I would come back and this woman would still look the same, act the same and be the same. That the years spent away would not age her or change her. I placed all my hope into the belief that everything would be frozen in time until I came back and picked up where we left off. I stood up next to her, placed my hand on her head and pressed it against my side as I bent down to kiss her forehead. "*Cuando te vas mijo*?' she asked.

"Wednesday grandma." I replied.

She gripped my hand in hers and for a moment I was a child again, safe in her grasp, knowing she would take care of me. Her love would protect me. She sat there as I stroked her hair, now showing more signs of gray. I stood in silence as she began to rock back and forth slowly, her head against me, starting to weep. It seemed like forever although it could not have been more than a minute. A long lonely minute in silence embracing the sadness of not knowing when we would both feel this close again.

She was losing her young man to life. I would not be coming back to the sameness of things no matter how much I believed I would. She knew this better than I did and I don't believe she was ready to let go.

"I'll write you grandma," was all I could get out of my mouth as a tear from my cheek found its way onto her forehead. I reached around and grabbed both her arms now locked around my waist as tight as I had ever felt them. Her grip eased a bit since she knew it was time. I wiped the tears from my eye and reached down to give her a last kiss on the forehead as her eyes moistened from the tears.

She didn't say a word and only stared ahead to some far off place she went to when she needed to gather strength. As I turned towards the door and reached for the handle, I heard her low soft whimper break the silence of the moment. "I love you *cabroncito, no se te olvide,* " she cried. The rush of emotion was too much to bear as I could only raise my hand in the air to acknowledge what she had said, too broken up to reply.

# CHAPTER ELEVEN

"Ladies and Gentlemen I don't know if you realize this about our guest of honor here tonight but as a child, he was an altar boy in the Catholic Church. Well, let me tell you something, I'd been his partner for the last six years and all I can say is - GO TO CONFESSION AND PLEAD FOR MERCY!" exclaimed Victor as everyone in the audience laughed. He looked over at me and grinned.

I could tell the tequila had done its job and transformed him into the local version of Paul Rodriguez. Victor was losing his hair and gained a few pounds. Lately he was even starting to look like him. The ceremony had begun and as master of ceremonies, Victor set the mood for everyone to follow. I don't know if all retirement functions go as this one seemed to be heading, but I knew I was to be mercilessly roasted. I figured my best approach should be to grin and bear it then wait till the end to get my revenge during the farewell speech. I knew no one there would be cruel and everything said would be in jest. To me it was better than getting into truly emotional speeches, which always made me feel so uncomfortable.

It is touching to me when a person expresses gratitude for having worked with me or has gained something from knowing me as a person. But the mushy heartfelt feelings expressed in words are difficult for me to endure simply because they get to me. I didn't wish to get emotional when it came time for me to speak.

"And now ladies and gentlemen there are various people who wish to say a few words also. I wish to start off at this time with Mr. Bob Smith from Washington D.C. who is Director of the task group." "Mr. Smith if you would please…

I never really liked Bob Smith. He was a condescending man whose only reason for being here was obligatory. Sent down to satisfy the company edict of having someone there to say they gave a shit about you.

Perhaps this was a bit overboard but I knew he wasn't there because of his good-hearted nature. He and I had butted heads before on many issues. I knew how he felt about me just as he knew how I felt about him. Still, he had a tendency to talk and Victor was obligated to give him his turn to speak. Victor scheduled him first to get in and then out as soon as possible. He was a very good speaker but what he didn't understand was that people didn't like him simply because he was not a nice person.

Like grandma always said *Orgullo falso no se pemite!*

Protocol being what it is, I pretended interest in what he was saying up on the podium as my mind again drifted away to another time and place. After three years away in the military, I had returned home to El Paso. I realized how much things had changed. Everyone had changed. I had changed. Long gone was the immature nineteen-year-old that had left three years earlier.

I was a father and a husband now, more in tune with my responsibilities and my obligations. I came back and saw those who had raised me in a far more different light. I no longer felt like the unknowing child of their group. I was now an adult within their world with an equal say in the hierarchy. The next generation entrusted to be the glue that helps keep the family together.

I was still a student expected to learn from the elders. I could see that this was part of the cycle of family, the inevitable evolution of members from one generation to another. The older ones are still considered masters of the group but soon their tenures begin to give in to the advance of time. I don't know how other cultures handled it, but in *familias Mejicanas*, you are taught to respect the wisdom that comes with age. Elders possess wisdom and knowledge garnered from their many years of life. Wisdom comes as the result of prejudices endured. Lessons are empowered into knowledge by the pitfalls and the tragedies of life, to be passed on from one generation to the next. Stories that speak of sorrow and the pain, the joy and the hurt and the testament of *aguante!* That which is truly the essence of being Hispano.

Once, we were visiting my grandmother's house a couple of weeks after I had returned home and we had brought the baby over for my grandmother to see. The baby was a little over a year old now and my grandmother had not seen her since our return from California. My mother and father were there, beaming as proud grandparents. After a while, my father, my grandpa Joe and myself went outside for a beer and a smoke while the women stayed inside marveling at all the little things babies do.

Whenever I heard my father and my grandfather speak of this thing called *aguante*, they would say it with a conviction that comes from many a horror story of survival.

"*Mira mijo*," grandpa Jose would say, "*aguante viene de acá bajo*! *Aguante* is what makes you survive. It is what gives you character *porque eres mejicano, aahhuua*!"

He would grab his balls with his right hand while a beer can rested in his left. My father would nod his head in agreement to this testament.

"*La vida vale madre sin sufrir*," my father would say, "*Sin sufrir no es vida, verdad Macho*".

My grandfather would also nod in agreement. Jose had become my grandmother's third husband. He was a kind-hearted man whom everyone called Macho. They called him this because he had worked for the Southern Pacific Railroad and retired from there after forty-four years of service. He started out as a cabin sweeper back in the forties when the only job available to Mejicanos was cleaning passenger train cars when they pulled into the old Union Depot station in El Paso. He rose to the position of brakeman whose job it was to turn the handles that switched the train tracks from one line to the other. This made him strong and put muscles on his arms that could choke a bull. He stood six feet tall and had massive upper arms from working with steel so much. Pushing and pulling gears and moving trains from track to track. The reason they called him Macho was because his arms looked like sledgehammers. He was a kind and gentle man who had met my grandmother upon one of her return trips from California.

Every summer, my grandmother would go out and visit with the family still out west and spend a month or two out there. She made it a point to visit her brothers and sisters and all her nieces and nephews would come out and see her because they knew she was great fun to be around. Of course, whenever Lencha came to town there was sure to be a party. It was expected of her to stay with her two daughters and see all her grandchildren both in Los Angeles and San Francisco. So she spent a lot of time cruising up and down the Golden State, seeing all the families and relatives out there.

She would spend two or three nights at one family member's house and then move on to someone else's house. They would then throw another great *pachanga* with food and drink and parties that went on all night because Lencha was here from El Paso. Everyone wanted to spend time and drink with her. They knew she would get tipsy and say the silliest things and laugh and sing and tell stories about the old days. She would tell how her brothers had been young once and acted like fools. She would tell how their mothers had been in love with those same fools and how they had married. My cousins all wanted to listen to the stories since their parents never told them. It made them happy to know that their parents were once young and foolish. They loved to hear stories about the old days and their wild escapades. It helped them appreciate the sacrifices their parents had gone through and brought them together as family should be. This is what my grandmother's visits meant to them and why they appreciated seeing her every summer. My grandmother never cared if she embarrassed her brothers and sisters. She was who she was and she never meant to deliberately embarrass anyone outright. She loved to laugh with others and have them laugh at themselves.

She always said, "*Al que no le pestan los pies no se ha olido.*" It was her way of letting people know not to think they were better than anyone else was.

She had this way of making fun of you, laughing with you but not at you. No one was above reproach. She made fun of everyone, just as everyone made fun of her. She would howl with a laugh that could fill a room and was so infectious that the sourest person in the world could not help but join in. The only thing that ever really upset her was when someone felt they were too uppity to laugh at themselves. When she thought someone was out to spite her because she was female or because of the color of her skin that's when she really tore into someone.

One summer there, my grandmother went with my aunt Josefina to a grocery store in Los Angeles to buy groceries. They were looking for mangos in the vegetable section, which were hard to find. When she couldn't find them, she approached a clerk to ask him where they could be found. My cousin Lily had gone with both of them and she tagged along with my grandma in search of the elusive mangos. She tells the story about how they approached one of the clerks who was taking lettuce out of a box on the floor and stacking it up for display. As Lily tells it, the guy was a white guy although he appeared to be of European descent. He had black hair with a thick black mustache and dark features that made him look Italian. My grandmother approached him and in a very polite and appropriate manner and asked where the mangos were located.

She approached him and asked him in Spanish "*Oiga, donde tiene los mangos de venta*?"

The clerk, apparently in no mood to help anybody, looked her in the eyes and said " I DON'T SPEAK THAT SPANISH SHIT." He tried to wave her off with that "don't bother me now I'm too busy" attitude. He went back to pulling out heads of lettuce from the box on the floor.

My grandmother calmly but firmly puts her foot into the box of lettuce and stomps down hard on his hand that's grabbing for a head of lettuce as he yells out in pain. When the clerk rises with a half a head of lettuce in his hand, he has that goofy surprised look on his face. My *abuela* takes the lettuce out of his hands, puts it smack in front of his face and tells him in her best broken English, "You understand what stick this up your ass means *cabron*?"

She proceeds to take the lettuce in one hand while she uses the other to pull open the white smock the guy is wearing. She takes the head of lettuce and places it between his shirt and the smock and crushes it into his chest. My cousin Lily stands there with a look of shock on her face and only lets out a small laugh. She says the guy just stood there too shocked to say anything while my grandmother proceeded to cuss him out in Spanish.

The customers around them just gawk at this 5 foot 2 inch lady who has just crushed a head of lettuce into a clerk who is standing there with a look of shock on his face. All they can hear are scattered words of English here and there but no one, other than my cousin Lily who is now in stitches, has any idea what the hell is going on.

"Don't you know how to respect your elders *cabron*? I am a lady *que te va hechar la pompa a andar*. You respect me no matter what *chavalo mocoso, me entiendes*?"

The clerk, obviously regretting now that this woman ever walked into the store, is obviously thinking that waving off this small Mexican woman had been a bad move all around. Still not understanding a word of Spanish, he nevertheless nods his head in agreement to this last barrage of insults hurled by my grandma. I guess he understands the text of the words being said and "YES" was all he was able to get out of his mouth. He keeps bobbing his head up and down, mesmerized by the old lady's words.

*"Chavalo mocoso,"* exults my grandmother and with that turns and strides away from the produce section, not having found any mangos but obviously having found a strong dose of dignity.

One particular summer and as it just so happened upon her return from the California trip when the infamous "Safeway store incident" had occurred as it came to be known in family history, she met my Grandpa Joe. Their first encounter was at Union Station when Grandpa Joe's train pulled into El Paso arriving from Houston.

Her second husband Fidel had died two years earlier so my grandmother now made the trips out west by herself. Even in her older age, she was still a stunningly beautiful woman with a shapely figure and long black hair stretching down to her shoulders. She liked it long because it still gave the impression of a much younger looking woman. She could still turn it on with her large dark eyes that glowed with her smile and the smattering of red blush that made her cheeks look like soft roses. She was no match for the man they called Macho.

My grandma's train had stopped in Tucson on the way back from LA. In the confusion of loading and unloading baggage, her bags had been left somewhere in Arizona. My Grandpa Joe loved telling me the story about how he was exiting the caboose of his train that was parked next to the just arrived California express train. He says he'd seen her standing there looking at the suitcases laid out on the platform. As he rounded the corner, he remembered seeing a shapely woman looking very sophisticated with a summer hat on, hands on her hips, talking to the black porter who had trouble understanding what she was trying to say in her broken English.

"Is red with a black *garadora*, UUMM…how you say aahh…she said trying to remember the correct word for handle.

"*GARADORA*?..exclaimed the porter. "Lady what the hell is a *garadora*"?

My grandmother, not knowing too many English words but certainly understanding what the word "hell" meant, finally gave in to her upbringing. She bypassed the proper English phrases to get her point across

"Is a *garadora*, where you *garar la maleta, es Negro como tu,* she said as she gestures her hand in a grab and hold motion and points to him. She started dabbing her finger on the back of his hand to accentuate talking about his skin color."

"OOOHHHH! Red suitcase with a black handle right?" says the porter.

"Jes, Si, Thas right, black handle," says my grandmother who stands there smiling at the man smiling right back, both as happy as if they had discovered the cure for cancer.

*Le puedo ayudar*?" asked my Grandpa Joe as he came upon both of them still smiling and nodding their heads at each other. "Can I help you with something?"

Hey Clarence, how are you?" he asks the porter. Grandpa Joe tried to impress her by showing his command of the English language he had learned from years of working with the *gabachos* on the train crews. On long journeys from Texas to California and beyond, train crews had to speak to each other and learn to communicate. Not knowing the others language was not going to cut it.

"Hey Joe, how you doin," replied Clarence. "Just helping the lady here," he said as he went about trying to locate the red suitcase with the black handle.

To hear my Grandpa Joe say it, he said he could see she was impressed with him. To hear my grandmother tell the same story, she says she could tell he was smitten with her. Both tell two different perspectives on the same story but I believe they both felt the *chingaso* of love for each other at the same time on that day.

"*Si, por favor le puedes decir al Sr. que no encuentro mi maleta*," says my grandmother to Grandpa Joe as she smiled.

Grandpa Joe says when he looked at her face, he was lost in eyes that glowed as the moon on a clear desert night. He was off in a trance from a smile that made her whole face beam. It broke only when her fluttering eyebrows brought him back to the here and now.

On her part, she claims she had never seen such a tall handsome man with dark features and strong arms. It made her think of Javier Solis, the famous Mexican singer of that era who was sweeping away female hearts in

Mexico at the time.

"*Estaba bien machin como un matachín,*" she would say and laugh when they spoke about the time they first met on that platform. I believe she truly felt she had finally found the right one on the third try. He made her very happy for many years.

She could still be her domineering self at times but he had such a good heart that he would tolerate her ways by bending to her will. Though sometimes he would stand up to her and tell her not to act that way and that made her mad. But she would catch herself and put up that coy smile of hers and flutter her eyes and would defer to his wishes. They had a very strained yet romantic relationship. They would dance with each other in words and in spirit. He, the tall handsome man with a soothing nature, tough with others but gentlemanly around her. She with her soft beautiful *Azteca* features that drew him in like a spider into its web.

It was a union of dance that moved to a beat between stubbornness and compromise but with outbursts of shout that moved to a reserved peace. They truly loved each other. He was as happy with her free spirit as he was angry at her being so hard headed. She was happy with his strength as she was agitated by his calm approach to everything. They made quite a pair but maintained their steadiness in life by feeding off each other. I learned that what one lacked, the other fulfilled. At the time, I remember hoping that someday my life would be filled with the movements from this dance.

This is the view I had of my grandmother's life as I returned home from military service in the mid seventies. She was a step slower now, grayer and a little heavier but as spry as ever. I noticed she was more cautious in her perception of things. She still spoke her mind to others but with a stronger sense of awareness with her words. She was not as loud and boisterous as before but more subtle and direct. She didn't drink as much or should I say she didn't drink as frequently as before. She still smoked however.

She was in her late fifties now and I like to think that wisdom had been the impetus for this change in her. When I asked her if she thought this was true, she told me it was probably gas. *AAY Abuela!*

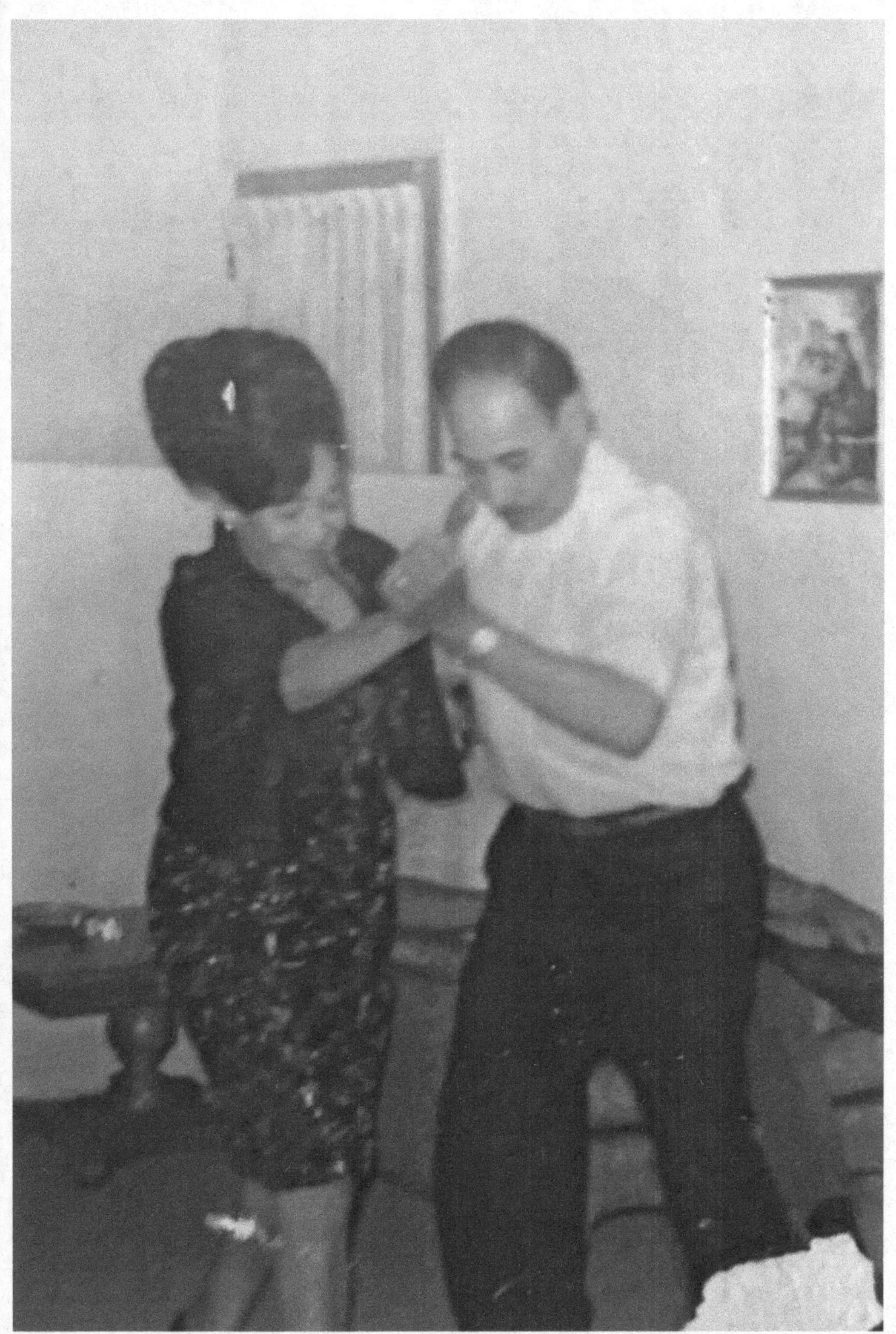

# CHAPTER TWELVE

I had rented a small apartment on the near east side and started the task of setting up a house for my wife and child. My ideals had changed and though I had the freedom to make decisions that would determine the direction my life would take, I also knew that the results from those decisions would be mine to bear. Adulthood brings the perils of bad decisions squarely onto one's own shoulders. No more claiming to be ignorant as I had done before my venture into the military. In my youth I could blame blissful ignorance and feel comfortable in allowing someone else to make a decision, one that I could complied with or chose to ignore. When I would benefit, ignorance praised my instincts for its success. If it went wrong, I claimed not to understand and figured I screwed up due to someone else's fault. Now I accepted the premise of responsibility and came to realize the error of my previous way of thinking. I had enough faith in myself to rely on my own instincts and realized the lessons my mother and my grandmother had taught me were making sense. In my attempt to make it through the time, that is early adulthood, I vowed to take things slow and think before I act. Still I came to rely on those who had been there before, offering me the benefit of their knowledge.

My abuela had told me that maturity is determined by how you come to understand it. This statement had intrigued me and I sought to discuss this with my grandmother. It was a couple of days before Christmas and she had asked me to take her to the supermarket to buy the *masa* to make tamales. She made damn good tamales and every year there would be a variety to choose from. There were her *tamales de chile colorado con pollo* that when she cooked them, the red *chile* brewed on the stove and filled the house with the pungent aroma of home. There were *tamales de frijol* mixed with cheese and chorizo that were so filling you could only eat a couple, and her tamales de chile verde con queso were so hot, they made you sweat because they were so *picosos*. But you didn't care, you still ate them because they were really good and the melted cheese gave it that just so flavor that melted in the back of your mouth. A few hours later though, you were obliged to make the painful yet mandatory visit to the bathroom where Montezuma's revenge led to a complete cleansing of the intestinal tract because of that *chile picoso*. Those were my personal favorites and she always made a couple of dozen extra of those. She also made *tamales de dulce* with sugar and raisins that went down as a sweet treat. Around Christmas, we ate tamales as a meal and tamales for dessert. No wonder my tio Manuel started to look like Bozo the clown.

"*Abuela*, when you need to make a decision, how do you know if you're making the right one?" We were at the Mercado now looking at the chicken and the finely packaged beef packets to find just the right ones to include in her recipe. I was pushing the shopping cart behind her as she was busy sizing up which ones to select for the tamales. She stopped and looked at me, brimming with one of those smiles of wisdom. The kind someone gives you when they realize you're finally starting to understand things.

"*Mijo*, just by asking that question proves you have the sense to make the right decision. *Muchas veces mucha gente* don't want to admit they don't have the answers to everything. She said in her own brand of Spanglish, "They think it is a sign of weakness if you reach out and ask for *ayuda* from someone else. *Eso no es bueno mijo porque* not everyone knows the right answer to everything. When you admit to yourself you don't know everything, this will help you find the right direction," she said as my mind kept racing from English to Spanish.

The Mejicanos across the border call those of us born on this side "pochos". This was a derogatory term meant to single us out as not being quite Mexican and not quite American. Only pochos spoke Spanglish, a mixture of both languages blended into common sentences depending on which got to the point the quickest and easiest way. Even people like my *abuela* who had been steeped in the Spanish language, yet exposed to English spoken in the border area picked up these phrases. It didn't bother me being called a pocho. Better a pocho than a *mojado* I thought.

"*Acuerdate mijo*" continued my abuela, " Never be too proud to ask for advice from those who have been here longer than you. This is what *familia* is about. Don't be stubborn like your *tios* and those *cabrones* that are too *Mejicaniados*. They were raised in Mejico to be stubborn and there is nothing worse than a stubborn Mejicano."

She picked up the chicken that met her satisfaction and we made our way over to the *chile* section where the finest green and red chile pods would find their way into her special recipe. I could tell she enjoyed the opportunity to relay her wisdom to me in her older age and so did I.

"*Este tiempo* is very important en *tu vida* and you have to listen before you act *porque* when you are *ayteen* you know everything there is to know, then when you turn thirty, you suddenly think you know everything," she was in the vegetable section surrounded by the red *chile* pods that were strung together in a circle. They were hung as a decoration piece outside homes at this time of year in the old Spanish tradition. In her element and quite at home, she was tossing out ugly looking *chiles,* Then she said, "but when you turn forty, you realize you don't know SHIT," not even blinking an eye and never looking up from her search for the perfect *chile.*

At the time of this revelation, it did not make sense to me but since I turned forty, I have come to fully understand this statement. This is the one I always remember from her. It was prophetic yet so simple in its message and all these years later, I found it to be true. It was something I now try to pass on to my granddaughters with the same logic and explanation that *abuela* had given me. Yet, the best I can do is hope they understand its meaning someday and pray that time allows them the patience to prove it in life.

All these years later, as I now sit here pretending to be interested in what Ron Smith was now mercifully saying, "and in conclusion…" I remembered that day at the Mercado and how she had been so right about maturity and understanding. How one must not allow ignorance to rule your thoughts. Pride has always been a staple in the Mejicanos way of thinking but pride is a direct descendant of ignorance. When applied to situations, it leads to a wrong decision since the decision comes at a time when one is stubborn. Not everyone got it, as was evident by the gringo now standing up at the podium talking.

I forced a smile as I reached out to shake his extended hand as he awarded me a plaque with gold lettering on it and presented me with the letter signed by none other than the Attorney General of the United States of America.

Don't get me wrong, I was grateful for the recognition. It had been an honor to serve my country as a civilian as it had been to serve in my military capacity. But it was the end of a long and successful period of service to my country. I was reflecting on this period and coming to understand the long journey here. What it took to get here and who was responsible for me being here. People were there to pay homage to a stellar career but if anyone deserved credit for all the accomplishments noted tonight, it was those that helped me get here.

Aside from my own initiative, it was only appropriate to recognize those who had helped me make it. To them I would owe a debt of gratitude since they were the ones that got me to this point in my life. In all the lessons and all the experiences, the end had justified the means. I owed them this recognition plus so much more. Although my name was inscribed on all the plaques and letters so ceremoniously presented to me today, I was the end result of all those not here anymore. I stand here today, humbled by their tutoring and their efforts.

"Thank you Mr. Smith, I appreciate this award," I said as I held up the plaque and smiled for the photographer who was hired to record the Kodak moments of this auspicious occasion. I took my seat back on the dais as Victor again rose to introduce the next speaker. I could not help but recall all those special moments in my life that now flooded back to me, triggered by a simple question posed by my partner earlier tonight. So many memories, so many lessons learned from an invaluable journey through life.

My body felt warm from the appreciation expressed by so many. My head started to relay the thought that it was time for a form of expression. Immediately that well known lump-in-the-throat syndrome started to tighten around my vocal cords signaling the onset of tears. But I would not allow that. It was not in me to relieve myself this way since there were still others to follow. The thought of me crying right now would be cause for the crowd to imitate this feeling starting to overcome me. I was scared that by the time it came to speak, I would be a blubbering idiot, crying his eyes out with everyone in the audience doing the same thing leaving a room full of cry babies. Anyone walking in would wonder what the hell was going on with so many blithering idiots crying and me leading the pack.

Besides, although I was a retired federal agent, I was still a *vato* from the barrio at heart and the others would not allow me to live the moment down. I could just hear them making fun of the ceremony and I did not want to be the butt of those jokes. I focused again on the strength my grandmother had instilled in me. I remembered how I always saw her pull strength up from the center of her body somewhere and somehow willed herself to be strong.

I recall that as a child I had wanted to escape my life. I wanted to live the life I perceived as normal, that which I saw on television. Every time I watched "Leave It To Beaver," I imagined the Anglo mother with the petticoat dress and high heels and the apron on was my mother. When I saw the house they lived in or the one that Ozzie and Harriett lived in, I imagined myself coming down the stairs in those nice pressed shirts and pressed jeans with my hair combed in just that certain *gavacho* way. The lawns outside the houses looked well manicured and the whole neighborhood appeared nice and clean and plenty of food was evident when they sat down to dinner. They would all talk politely to each other. The parents would ask the children how their day went and oh, everything looked so perfect. I would imagine myself seated next to the Beaver as he recounted the crazy situations that he and his best friend (Whitey, the chubby little white kid) got into that day. We would joke and laugh and wonder how two boys could get into so much trouble. Oh, that Beaver!

Instead dinners at my house consisted of *gritos* and complaints, *"frijoles otra vez! "UGH*!" My mother did not appreciate this and it would make her very angry when anyone complained. *"PUES AQUI NO ES RESTORANTE, SI NO LES GUSTA VAYAN Y COMAN CACA! DESGRACIADOS!"* Whatever we had was because that's all we could afford to have. Looking back now, I should have been more appreciative. My younger brother and I would be eating a plate *of papas and frijoles con tortilla.* We had a small, very small kitchen table that doubled as a business desk along with a place to eat. My mother reviewed and paid the bills on it so papers were always stuffed into those cheap paper holders that you buy in Mexico from some guy on the street that cost a dollar. There were boxes of ready to make *atole* (oatmeal) and bottles of Louisiana hot sauce and the phone book on top and two or three bottles of *tequila Sauza* all pushed over to the side of the table next to the wall along with various newspapers and magazines. My mothers purse was stacked on top of the whole mess. This didn't leave a whole lot of room at the table to eat, so we ate our meals in semi-shifts with my father, of course, in the first wave seeing as he was the breadwinner of the family.

My sisters were accounted for at each sitting except on those special days when two of them would sit together. This mercilessly left only one to deal with, err.., I mean to enjoy dinner with. My mother usually sat with my father as would be appropriate so we never really got a chance to eat as a family. No one really asked how anyone else's day went and generally I only recall a lot of arguing about who did what or whose fault this or that was. There were occasional spurts of yelling coming from my mother or father telling us to be quiet. "*Callense y coman o ahorita mismo les doy un jalon de mechas.*" There was that *jalon de mechas* saying again. I still didn't know what it meant and wasn't anxious to find out.

Dinners at my grandmother's were more boisterous and chaotic. There was a constant upheaval of people sitting down or standing up to eat. There were always two or three conversations going on between people standing and drinking and people sitting and eating. You couldn't figure out who said what or keep any stories straight. If you got up to get something else chances were you lost your seat. Your plate would be shoved aside and upon your return would be handed it and told to finish eating someplace else, you're out.

Seeing as how this was usually done by an older member of the family or at times someone too drunk trying to sober up by eating, it was best to follow the advice given. After all, I did not start growing to a formidable size until I turned thirteen. Then I became one of those who told the smaller family members to go eat someplace else. Looking back now though, I'm glad I grew up the way I did. I came to understand that with the hard times, the confrontations and family crisis that I went through, it prepared me for what I experienced in the future. I was better equipped than others for the tough times I endured. It gave me a better understanding of my interactions with others. My family's insanity brought me my sanity. To me there was no one tougher in mind and strength than my grandmother. Anyone I met after her was strictly kid's stuff. If I could survive her and overcome the racism I experienced as a young Mexican American, I could survive anything.

This was my passage to adulthood. A gift of understanding that taught me to learn the hard lessons life brought onto you. If you understood them you would be assured of survival in this society. My mother who never exhibited the rougher and more aggressive side her mother had come to master, had her own subtle way in which to exhibit this same attribute. From one I learned that at times, one needs to speak in a loud and tenacious voice. From the other, I learned that one needs only apply a dominating stare to express disapproval. My mother had an icy stare that could shake me to the core of my soul. Indeed I had been on the receiving end of the two methods expressed and had endured their effects on my conscience. A feeling I would avoid if at all possible.

Yet, the two women had also shown me the beauty of life. They helped me appreciate how to treat a woman. They showed me the beauty of a woman both inside and out. I was taught the meaning of respect and how it was expected of me to act as a man of courage. Not by domination and ignorance, but by listening and being mindful.

I learned to tolerate and empathize, to hold steady and apply firmness when deemed necessary. I had wanted to escape this life as a child yet by doing so I would have been running away from the very substance that made me. To run away from one's self is impossible. When you understand yourself first as the person you are, then and only then can you understand anyone else. The one thing however that still bothered me was the relationship I found myself in between these two special women.

I set out to find if this feeling of being uncomfortable was just a figment of my imagination or if there really was something to it. I searched out my mother one day to ask if this was just a delusion on my part. Better to face a fact I thought than to drive yourself crazy thinking something was there when there isn't. There were a couple of times before I had left for the Service that I asked my grandmother about it. She would always respond by saying I was her grandson and that she loved me very much but both times

I had seen the expression on her face say something else. Something in her face always told me there was something she wasn't saying. I didn't think much of it but now as an adult, I began to bring into view issues that now seemed clearer to me. I found that there were things from my youth that still bothered me.

"*Mijo*, aren't you supposed to be in school, I thought you had class on Wednesday *por la noche*," asked my mother. I had planned on stopping by right after my sociology class on Wednesday nights. A quiz was scheduled but we were told that Mr. Chavez the instructor had been called out of town on an emergency. Class was canceled for the night so even better, I thought. This gave me the chance to go to my mother's house earlier than I had planned.

"No, *es que* it got canceled for today," I said in my El Paso Spanglish. Damn, I would have to start breaking that habit and speak either full English or full Spanish. "How are you mama? *Como estas*?" I pulled out the kitchen chair next to the little table where we spent so many shift dinners. Now that my younger brother had gone off to California to work, my parents were by themselves in the small house that now appeared just the right size for two people.

I found it hard to believe that at one time, nine people had lived in this small home. My parents, brothers, sisters and I all spent a lot of life in this house. It seemed smaller and smaller to me every time I stopped by now. The kitchen table was still stacked with yesterday's newspaper, mail and assorted papers as it had always been. There was a box of lemon cookies on the table. My mother was sitting across from me in the only other chair, playing solitaire. My father was in the next room watching his favorite show, "Green Acres" on television.

He was such a stoic faced man. The only times I remember him laughing was when that show was on. It used to be "the Beverly Hillbillies" before but now the pig they called Arnold Ziffel was making him laugh. He sat in front of the tube mesmerized by the corny lines and acknowledged my entrance by a wave of his hand in the air. I knew he would be in his own zone and this would be a good time to talk to my mother.

My mother was at ease when she played cards. She learned to play from her mother who learned it from the railroad workers all those years before. I in turn had learned it from her along with every other card game imaginable. My mother played a mean game of poker. Rarely did I beat her at it. She, after all, had learned it from the best. I enjoyed the few times we would play together.

"*Vente mijo*, let me deal and let's play blackjack" she said as she gathered the cards to shuffle.

"OK mama, wanna beer?" I asked and leaned over to open the refrigerator door. In such a small kitchen I had learned to tilt back and open the door while balancing myself precariously on the chair.

"Si hombre." She said, "*Y dame un shot de tequila de chaser*," She flashed her mischievous grin as I placed a cold one on the table before me. Long ago. when she had given birth to my older brother David at such a young age, she had given up drinking and smoking altogether. Her favorite vices were now pumpkin seeds, which she devoured by the ton. Sometimes I would go up to New Mexico and buy her ten pound bags of seeds sold on the side of the road at fruit stands and bring them back. They would be gone within a week's time. She didn't miss drinking or smoking. When we were at parties over at my grandmother's house, she would watch everyone else getting drunk on the booze. She always wondered how in the world she could have done that. My mother always complained about my father's drinking. She also preached to my grandmother about her vices, but she wasn't a pain about it. As the dutiful daughter, she always made sure my grandmother had a drink in hand and a smoke at the ready. Though after a while, she would tell my grandmother about the bad things she was doing to her body. My grandmother would wave her off saying she was already an old woman anyway. Life wasn't meant to be lived forever.

Here they were again. Two women in my life are so much alike yet so different. Mother and daughter with similar traits but very different characteristics. My grandmother was the more free spirited after having seen and lived through the hard times at such a young age and my mother, the dutiful daughter, the oldest of the siblings, was aware of her responsibilities to care for her mother. I could swear it appeared as if the roles between mother and daughter had been reversed. My mother was the responsible one and my grandmother was the carefree one. My grandmother wanted to get everything she could out of life, living it to its fullest.

My mother's idea of relaxing was playing cards after a long day of doing household chores, taking care of my father and tending to my grandmother's needs. Add to that seeing to my grandpa Joe and it made for a tiresome day. My grandmother was now in her mid sixties, putting my mother close to fifty-one. Life was starting to take a toll on her and she looked tired and drawn out. I was glad we were all out of the house now. There were less people to watch and care for.

"How come you always get to deal, you always get to be the house," I groused at her in a playful way as I popped the top on the beer can.

She scrunched her face at me and replied in her playful tone "My house, my rules *cabroncito.*" She was in a good mood. I thought it was a good time to approach her about my dilemma.

"Mama, can I ask you something?" I said.

"*Si* of course *mijo.*" She kept shuffling the cards, one over the other in a rhythm, all the while enjoying the moment.

"I'm going to ask you something but… first, I want you to know that I love you very much as my *jefita.* I am really proud to be your son." I didn't know how to begin this but figured I should first say something to reinforce my love for her. It didn't. Instead she froze in mid shuffle and looked at me with that *OH! OH!* look that meant she didn't know what to expect.

I guess all parents get like this when their children say something like that. She stared at me for a while. For some reason, I started getting nervous not really knowing how to phrase the question I wanted to ask. I needed to know why I had always felt like a pawn between her and her mother, flesh of her flesh, blood of her blood. Maybe I really didn't need to know any of this. Maybe I should just let things be as they are. Maybe... I shifted in my seat and took a swig of beer with one hand and wiped my lips with the other.

She gazed long and hard at me and said, "What *mijo*, don't tell me you're…turning *joto.. or como se dice…eres* GAY!" as she held her breath .

"WHAT! NO MAMA, ME! no , no I'm not …*shingado*..no, no." I shifted in my seat again and thought maybe this wasn't such a good idea. "No, mama, I just…just have something to ask you and I ...I don't know how to say it. I don't want you to get, you know, upset or anything." I took another swig of beer. I saw her eyes come back to normal with a relieved look on her face.

"*Ay dios mio, bendito sea dios*," she said as she crossed the holy trinity across her chest in relief. This was, after all, a woman born in the early part of this century. Although it was the late seventies, she still clung to her beliefs in the old fashioned ways.

"*Ayy gracias* a *dios hijo*, don't be putting…" she stopped in mid sentence and her eyes narrowed into a glare. "You're not getting divorced are you? "Did you find *otra mujer*?"

The tone in her voice was cold as she put down the deck of cards and crossed her arms in that, *WELL TELL ME,* posture that mothers do. "No, mama it's not that at all." I crossed my leg over and played with the cuff of my pant bottoms wishing I had never brought this up.

"*ENTONCES*! What, tell me." She said and remained in the imposing figure with her arms crossed across her chest waiting for a confession. I felt the way I used to as a kid when I got caught doing something wrong. Trying to find a way to weasel out of it. Wait a minute here, I thought to myself, I'm not a child anymore. What am I doing!

The best way to get through this was to be frank and say what's on my mind, getting straight to the point. I planted both feet firmly on the floor and crossed my hands on top of the table as I leaned forward. Maybe my conscience was secretly telling me to pray for help.

"*Es que*, I have always wondered mama, and I always wanted to ask you if there is...well…what is it between you and grandma when it comes to me? I always feel like I'm being pulled back and forth between both of you or something. Ever since I was *chiquito*, I felt she was pulling me one way and you would pull me another." I had been looking beyond her face while I said this. I finished my statement and focused on her face. Her expression went from inquisitive to a blank one. Kind of like when you say something to someone they didn't really want or expect to hear. Almost as if a look of resignation came over her face. She looked down. I knew I must have hit a nerve somewhere inside. I tried to retreat and make her feel less threatened.

"It's not that I really minded all these years mama," I said. "It's just that well… now I'm older and it's something I've always wondered about and... and…"

I took another swig of the beer . I looked over at my father, praying he wasn't listening in on our conversation. He wasn't. I could tell he was into the program. From the TV I could hear Mr. Haney talking to Mr. Douglas about buying farm equipment or something. My father just laughed and laughed. He was off into the world of Green Acres.

I returned to the conversation, "and I just always wondered if it was just me or whether I did something wrong one time and you had to cover for me or….*pues no se*…I just always felt like that and I just wondered why. Me *entiendes* mama, you know what I mean?" There was a silence that remained for what seemed like forever but couldn't have been more than a minute. I saw she was staring at the table but in her mind she was away in some far off place thinking. She picked up the deck of cards just as I was about to say, "you know what, just forget I ever brought it up."

Her gaze slowly came up to my eyes. I darted away from her stare thinking once again, why the hell did I bring this up. But my eyes again met hers.

I saw a look of comfort in them, the look a mother has for her child.

"*Pues si mijo, esta bien.* If you want to know the truth, *yo te lo dire.*" She went back and focused on the cards in hand as she laid the deck on the table. She tapped it slightly signifying she wanted me to break the deck. I picked it up in the middle and laid another deck next to it making two stacks. She picked one over the other and started to shuffle the cards. Not really into them anymore, her mind in some far away place.

*Hace yo creo* almost twenty years ago, en el 1960, something happened that affected us all," she said. Her mind now drifted off and she looked over at my father who was staring at the glow of the TV with its humor and enlightenment. "And you're right *mijo*. You are old enough now to know the truth. Es *importante saber la verdad*." Her eyes met mine. She gave a soft look and smiled ever so gently.

"Look mama," I said. "If it's something personal or something you don't want to talk about, I..."

"No, no, is OK, is OK," she interrupted. "I don't mind telling you *porque* you should know."

She glanced again at my father as she sat upright in her chair and placed the cards back on the table. "Remember when we would look through family pictures and I would show you photos of your tio Antonio?"

"Of course," I nodded. "He was in those pictures with my tio Manuel and you when you guys were all little."

"MMM…" she murmured, showing her affirmation. "Well, I know all of you have always asked what happened to him and we always said that he died in a car accident." She shuffled the cards nervously.

"That's not the truth. *La verdad es que* he died a very violent death." She put the cards down and was now playing with her wedding ring as she did whenever she was nervous about something. I started to have doubts about continuing this since I didn't know what the facts of the story were. But we had already started and I sure wanted to finish. I reached over and touched her hands.

"Go on mama," I said in a gentle voice.

"Well," she smiled, "your tio was a very fine looking man. He was a very handsome *hombre* with a joyous attitude towards life. He was always whistling and smiling. And he was always in a good mood for whatever reason. Ever since we were teenagers, he always attracted women because he would make them laugh. With those handsome eyes and jet black hair… oooh...he was something to look at. All my friends would always want me to introduce him to them. Sometimes it was all they would talk about. *Ay que Antonio esto, y Antonio el otro, y para ya, y para acá y...ay…*" She was fanning her arms in a back and forth motion, remembering the moments.

My tio Antonio had been the baby of the family group. My mother being the oldest always held a special place in her heart for him. She was left in charge when they were growing up and she took care of the baby as if he was her very own. When my grandmother would go to work her bartender job, my mother would care for her little brother as a mother cares for her infant. She herself was of a young age and my sister had told me once that my mother had admitted that her baby brother was the most special of all. She cared for him as a mother but treated him like a little play doll, dressing him, coddling him and feeling the joy of being around him. They were very close and everyone in the family knew this. My older sisters told me they remembered him being very close to my mother and would come around to the house a lot.

I didn't know where this story was going, but I could see it was tough on her. A tear appeared in the corner of her eye as she finished waving her hands in the air. I tore off a piece of paper towel from the cheap stand at the end of the table. She took it and dabbed her face, "They all wanted to meet him. All my *amigas* thought he was so handsome." She smiled as in her mind she remembered his face. "Anyway, Antonio met and married this girl named Linda, this beautiful girl he had met at school. They were both eighteen, madly in love and she was very good for him. She was a good-hearted woman, very *wuera* with blond hair and very beautiful. The other boys all wanted to beat Antonio up because he was the one all the girls wanted to go out with. Not those other *peleoneros*. Nobody wanted to go out with them so they would chase Antonio to try and beat him up. He was always too fast for them. Your tio Manuel and some of the others in the neighborhood,

Kikirica and Gordo, they would all help him if there was a fight.." At least now I knew why my grandmother always invited those guys from the neighborhood over to family functions at her house.

My mother continued, "so when Antonio turned twenty years old, he and Linda decided to marry. They lived in a little house close to where your father and I lived but down the road a ways. El Paso was just a small town then. Little Antonio was born and then Linda became pregnant with their second child. Antonio started working as a plumber for a company in town. I don't remember the name. Things were good then but then one day, he came to visit me at the house at a time when you were very, very sick. You were about six years old and you had developed a case of strep throat. *Ay mijo* ...you were so sick," she said as she kept folding the cards, one over the other. .

"So *despues*, when he came into the house, I knew he had something on his mind. He could always talk to me. Tell me anything, anything…" she wiped another tear from her eyes. It must have been tough on her to remember all the little details about the relationship with her little brother. I knew how much she missed him.

"He had this worried look on his face. I tried to get him to tell me what was wrong, but he wouldn't tell me. I begged him. I said, "Antonio *dime que tienes, déjame ayudarte por favor,"* her eyes welled up with tears as she recalled the events of that day.

My father looked over. He saw her crying and was about to get up to find out what was wrong but my mother waved him off with one hand. Showing him she was alright. He sat back down and went back into his TV trance.

"He kept telling me not to worry, that everything was OK. But I knew it wasn't. I don't know why but I just knew. He went over to where you were laying on the bed and sat next to you. He stroked your hair like this," my mother reached across the table and ran her hand gently through my hair, stroking my forehead and brushing the hair back in a comforting manner. "You were crying because your throat would hurt… *ayy* you were so sick *mijito*. I thought we might lose you there for a while."

My mother cupped my face in her hands. She hadn't done that to me in a long time and it felt good. I reached up and held her hands cradling my face. I smiled and she smiled back at me. Her face turned to sorrow as she continued with the story.

"He said you would be OK and you were. Those are the last words I remember hearing from him that day. He said you were a strong *chico* and that someday you would grow up and we would be very proud of you. He knew that you would be a good man. I don't know why he said that but while he was talking he kept stroking your face and then you stopped crying and drifted off to sleep. You looked so peaceful together. Antonio stroking your face and you asleep. *Ayy*... I can still see his face even today…" her voice trailed off as she stared into space. Her look then turned grim as she reached for another towel.

"He then got up, kissed me goodbye and left. I never saw him again. That night, the phone rang here about 2 in the morning. Tu papa answered it and it was tu *abuelita.* She was hysterical. The police were over there saying Antonio was dead. At least that's what she thought they were saying. I left you with your *hermanas* and *tu papa* and I dashed over to her house. We got there in time to see the sheriff handing the policeman a wallet that belonged to Antonio. I recognized it as his old leather wallet he always carried. The policeman was trying to calm your *abuela* down but once she saw the wallet, she screamed and she fainted."

My mother had always been a determined woman with the same look about her. She was not prone to emotional outbursts. She was a more reserved person, always showing a strong face when dealing with anything. Tonight she was showing me a side that I had never seen before. Her appearance was filled with anger coupled with anguish over the incident.

"The policeman said they found Antonio in a car parked out in the county on Zaragosa road. Shot a bullet through his head. They said he had committed suicide." My eyes locked on her as she told the story. She now turned to look at me with a deep glare.

> "My *hermanito* did not commit suicide!" She extorted. I had never seen this side of her. She was reliving the whole incident again as if it had happened yesterday.

"That is what they told us, but I know he did not do that to himself. For one thing he was left handed but they found the gun in his right hand. He was found with bruises on his face. But he looked fine when he showed up here at the house that afternoon." Her eyes softened as she caught her breath and returned to the present. Although many years had passed, the pain had dulled but had not completely left her.

"But in those days *mijo*, it was just another Mejicano killed. The *autoridades* were all a bunch of gringos that didn't care. We tried and tried to get them to investigate his death but they said no. They said their decision was final. They had a killing and they had a gun and that was the end of it."

My mother softened her grip on the cards and slowly let them fall onto the table, not really interested in playing anymore. She had this long drawn out look on her face that showed me she had learned to deal with the inevitability of it all. There had been no choice. She had never accepted the ruling in his death. She was right. In those days it was just another dead Mejicano. The gringos in power then didn't care. No one wanted to listen. It was the early sixties way back before the passage of the civil rights act and before the marches and the demonstrations. It was back when schools were still segregated and the gringos were the only ones with a badge. This was still considered the South, the southwest maybe but still the South.

"There was one other thing *mijo*," my mother said, her gaze drifting back to that horrible day. "They found another *mujer* in the passenger seat next to him, also shot dead. They said Antonio had killed her then killed himself.

A murder/suicide they called it. It was later discovered that la *mujer esa* was pregnant. That Antonio was the father and that their shame was something they could not live with. She, after all, was also a married woman."

She looked down at the floor and then up at the TV which was showing some commercial about the new 1979 model cars for sale.

"Perhaps that part I could believe," she sighed. "I know Antonio loved Linda very much just as she loved him. He would not have wanted her to go through the embarrassment of another woman claiming to have his child or have to deal with the fact that he had another child by someone else. He adored her and the children and would not have wanted to put them through that but *aayy*…I can just hear him. His charm and his wit made any woman instantly fall for him."

All these years later, I could tell she still missed him. "If it was true about the affair, then it was wrong. But I knew my *hermanito*. I know how charming he could be without knowing it. He was truly something, *dios lo tenga en paz*," my mother sighed as she made the cross of the trinity across her chest in remembrance.

"After his funeral," she continued, "Linda left El Paso and moved to California where the family helped her find a place to live and helped her settle down. My tio Chava and my tia Maggie always watched after her. At first, she would stay in touch and call me a couple of times a year. Until once, she told me it was very hard for her to talk to me. Too many memories for her to bear, she said. I told her I understood and to call me if she ever needed anything. Every now and then she sends me something when your *abuela* goes out to California to see her, a charm, a bracelet or something. Tu *abuela* says little Antonio is all grown up and married now and that Lydia is just as pretty and *wuera* as her mother."

My mother leaned over the table and took my hands in hers. "When this happened mijo, it was very hard on your grandmother and on me. It was very hard on me since I lost my baby brother. But to her, she had lost her baby boy. She never truly got over it and when you started growing up, you always seemed to be by her side. You are very good for your *abuela* and we always talk about how you have a lot of your tio's habits and gestures. We sometimes talk about what he said when you were sick in bed. Your *abuela* says he must have had a premonition about you. She sees a lot of him in you. You have many of his same features except he was not as tall as you are. But your *abuela* always tells me she sees many of Antonio's…*como se dice*... charatristiks."

"You mean characteristics mama." I said.

"*Aahh si, caratristiks de Antonio,"* she replied. She cupped my face in her hands again and said "*Mijo*, your *abuela* and I don't fight over you. Each of us sees something special in you because of who you are. To her you are the embodiment of my *hermanito* and you are also her grandson. She adores you for who you are but you also fulfill that emptiness she felt when my hermanito left. You are my son and I love you very much. I also love my *madre* and I like to see her happy. Although you were born unto me, I know you are special to us both. Your older brother David grew up very differently. If I had to do it over, perhaps I would have brought him with me so your father could raise him as we wanted to. I wanted to make my mother happy and I relented to her wishes. But you my *moreno*, you I will not give in on. And so we both entrust our love onto you for our own selfish reasons. I hope you understand that you stand for something very special to both of us. We are both getting to be old *viejas* and will not be here on this earth for many more years. Please understand how special you are to us both. I am the woman who bore you. She is the woman who influenced you. Never forget we both love you very much."

I did not know what to say. I could see a joy in her eyes that replaced the earlier feeling of anguish. She had made her peace with the events in her life and both women had an unspoken bond between them as a result of this tragedy. They were not just mother and daughter but survivors of the most difficult hurt of all, the loss of a child. A child they both helped raise.

I understand my role now. I saw my situation not as a burden but as a blessing. I was able to bring them happiness and comfort from a long ago incident. My mother was smiling now. I had not seen that smile on her face since my childhood. I thought it best not to say anything more. This was something I would do well to digest and to speak of when I came to better understand. I reached out and brought her head close to me and kissed her on the forehead.

For a moment, I truly felt a bond with my mother I would sadly never again feel. Words could not come to me as I rose from her grasp and stood before her. She wiped her eyes clean and cleared her throat as she went back to shuffling the deck of cards. Laying them out to set up another game of solitaire. I turned to wave at my father who had fallen asleep in front of the TV again just as the ten o'clock local news was starting to come on.

"*Buenas noches* mama", I said as I opened the kitchen door to the outside.

As always she said the same four words she said to everyone when we said goodbye. "*Que dios te lleve.*"

I opened the screen door and shut it behind me taking a last glance at her before I got into my truck. She was sitting there at the kitchen table, lost in thought by another game of solitaire

# CHAPTER THIRTEEN

The next few years were surprisingly calm. In the early eighties, I joined the federal government as an agent that required me to travel out of town on a semi-frequent basis. With the demands of the job and in my efforts at continuing my education at night, there was hardly enough time to spend quality time with the family. My daughter was growing up and I wanted so much to be a part of that. The strain to buy a piece of the American pie and purchase a home and get used to life in the suburbs took a lot of time and effort. I tried to keep night classes to a minimum to keep from burning myself out too fast. I attended one or two classes per semester and tried to keep classes down to two days a week. It made for long days spent at work in the day and in a classroom at night.

Weekends were spent fixing all the little home repair jobs around the house or spending time with the family. I considered school an important part of my life since I realized that education held the key to a better life. The holy grail of success was in the form of an education. Another influence was that my mother always expressed regret at never having completed her education. She had given up school to care for her siblings. She helped her mother out by working at small jobs to bring in money but her one regret in life was that she was never able to continue her studies.

Knowledge fascinated her. She always had an interest in the classes that formed my degree plan. She was always asking which particular class I was taking. When I'd tell her, she would want to know what it was about, what we were studying and why it was relevant. She seemed genuinely interested in the subject matter, always tapping my brain for an overview of the classes.

She found sociology particularly interesting since it seemed to her it was a study in ideology and beliefs. Once, I even did a report based deliberately on her upbringing. It was in a social science class that studied cause and effect on class structure when education is absent and the effects it has on that group as it enters adulthood. The paper exemplified the effects on a generation of individuals who by choice (or as I found was evident in the Mexican American generation born in the 1920's and 30s,) by necessity lacked the benefit of having had formal schooling past the 10th grade. In this category, the results were dismal. Very few had even reached this level of education at all. As the grade level climbed, so did the increase in the number of individuals that no longer attended. The number of Mexican Americans male and females from that generation with a fifth or sixth grade level of education was much higher than the number of individuals continuing school in the higher grades.

My mother's situation was a prevalent example of how Mexican Americans in her generation were forced to leave school due to family obligations or economic necessity. I found this to be a staggering fact among this age group. This was more the norm than the exception for her generation. Even my father had not progressed past the sixth grade for similar reasons. The opportunity to achieve educational parity with the Anglo class of their generation was sacrificed. Money in hand was the more crucial issue back then. Times were tough and everyone that could work had to work.

If anyone within the Hispanic family stood to reap the benefits of education, it would fall on their younger brothers and sisters. Hopefully they would be the lucky few to attend school to its completion. My parent's generation was entrusted with keeping the family together to allow them to survive. It goes without saying then that my mother pushed her children to continue to strive in their educational objectives. She knew what it meant to have sacrificed that goal so long ago.

This was what my pursuit of a higher education was all about so I continued to pursue my goal in achieving a college degree. I would discuss with my mother the teachings of the great society and debate the industrial revolution with her. How it had been going on while she was growing up working at the mills and while she worked the fountain shop at Woolworths. How she had been a part of this. She was fascinated by it all and I regret that I did not make more time to visit her more often to continue these discussions. But free time was becoming more and more of a rare commodity to me.

I began to notice a difference in the relationship between my grandma Lencha and my mother. Ever since that night when my mother told me the story of her brother Antonio, it appeared as if they had come closer together. I was certain that my mother had told grandma about our talk. I assumed this had opened up another chapter in their views over that period of time. Knowing them the way I did, I figured they must have talked and dredged out more emotions that helped heal rather than hurt. Years had passed and both of them came to grips with the events from the past in their own peculiar way. Ways in which they had come to share with each other. Also, perhaps it was the fact my grandmother was now getting noticeably older.

For a woman born in the very early part of the century, she was now well into facing her last years. Mentally she showed no signs of slowing down. Physically it was a different story. Age is an escort to us all in this journey through life. She was clearly starting to show its impact. Trips to the doctor were now becoming more and more frequent and my mother was the one responsible for getting her there. In any event, they seemed closer than ever now. At times my mother would ask us, her children, to help out whenever possible in meeting her medical obligations. Those of us living in El Paso would help out when asked and since my mother herself was not exactly a young woman either. We were all glad to oblige when we could.

My memories of these medical visits are a bit different because of two particular incidents that I recall. You see, my grandmother was now in her early seventies and years of hard work and a hard life had taken a toll on her physically. Although her mind was as clear as ever, the doctors wanted her to slow down some. They recommended she quit bad habits like staying up late, eating the wrong foods and of course her two worst vices, drinking and smoking. When doctors first told her to quit drinking and smoking, she was in her fifties. Even then she waved off the doctor as if they were speaking a foreign language. Essentially this was pretty much the truth. She had been with her first doctor, Dr. Chavez, since she was in her twenties. By the time the doctor was in his late sixties he was ready to give up his practice and retire. He was considerate enough to attempt to farm out his patients to other doctors based on their method of handling patients. This was pretty decent of him seeing as how he could just as easily have walked away and left everyone to fend for themselves. But Dr. Chavez was a pretty decent guy.

Growing up in El Paso you have a large Hispanic population that includes professionals in many categories. In the early days there were some doctors, though not many who spoke Spanish as their native tongue. Dr. Chavez was one of those who did. He had a clientele made up almost exclusively of Spanish speaking patients. My grandmother was very comfortable with him. No doubt it troubled her when he announced his retirement from practice but she understood his reasoning.

My mother, the dutiful daughter, was the one who took care of these things. My grandmother didn't concern herself with looking for a new doctor since that was my mothers job. What my grandmother didn't know was that Dr. Chavez intended to pass her on to a Korean doctor known as Dr. Lin Wei. Now, the good Mexican doctor had the righteous intentions because Dr. Wei did, in fact, turn out to be a very good doctor and a compassionate man. When my grandmother turned sixty-three, Chavez retired and referred her to Dr. Wei.

I had agreed to help my mother take my grandmother for her first scheduled visit to this new doctor. It was then that we discovered Dr. Wei did not speak very good Spanish. The good doctor requested a family member be available just in case he needed someone to interpret. I remember this being an old standard practice at many places in El Paso. The children of Spanish speaking Mejicanos were the interpreters for their parents many times then as today. Often, they found themselves as the only person in the house with a good grasp of English. Adults who were not proficient in the English language were left with little choice. Most times it fell on the young ones to translate something to or from the grocer, the insurance agent, teachers, police officers, everyone or anyone who had dealings with your parents or grandparents. This was no big deal to me.

My mother checked in at the front desk and the three of us sat down waiting to be called. Our turn came and I accompanied both of them into the exam room since my mother wasn't too comfortable with her English. I should have known things would get crazy when we were called in. My grandmother was in one of her sour moods. She had very little patience for anyone whose job it was to tell her what she could or couldn't do. A visit to the doctor was at the top of this list. The doctor walked in and he had my grandmother's rather thick medical history file with him.

"Good morning, I am Dr. Wei so nice to meet you." He said as he extended his hand.

My grandmother looked at him with a cautious gaze. "*Como? Como dice que se llama o que dice este guey*?" She said in her antagonist voice. My mothers face turned red from embarrassment.

"Yes, how are you? My name is Dr. Wei," he said again with his hand still extended.

"No *ama, su appellido es* Wei, *no le digas guey, aayyy,*" my mother's face turned a bright shade of red as she motioned my grandmother to take his hand and shake it.

My grandma Lencha reached out and shook it with only the slightest effort. *"Pues por eso te pregunto, como se llama este guey, yo no lo conozco! Dices que haci se llama verdad,* DR GUEY!" she says in a loud voice.

The doctor, not understanding Spanish but having heard his last name phonetically pronounced, then responds, "Yes, my name is Dr. Wei, nice to meet you too." He says as polite as possible.

My grandmother stares at him and apparently doesn't quite understand why this man keeps calling himself a bad word in Spanish. My mother and I, understanding the play on words between his last name and the slang word used on the street, try to act cool as if nothing is wrong though I hear her stifle a small laugh. The good doctor, of course, has no idea of the similarity in pronunciation between his name and the word used on the street. My grandmother, not knowing any better, looks at the doctor and asks "*y porque te dicen guey?"*

The doctor stands there studying her medical chart. When she asks him, he looks up at her again and says, "YES, I AM DR WEI," and goes back to studying her medical chart.

My grandmother, thinking that the good doctor understands Spanish again asks him "*Si, pero PORQUE te dicen guey, que estas pendejo o que*?"

My mother and I do not look at each other for fear of laughing out loud at watching this Abbott and Costello routine. It was too late. Her eyes looked at me, just as I looked at her to ask what the next move should be, and we both just lost it.

Meanwhile, the doctor again having heard my grandmother speak Spanish and hearing the pronunciation of his name again looks up from studying the medical file and says, "Yes Dr. Wei."

Again my grandmother says, "*Si ya se, pero porque te dicen guey*?"

He again looks up, smiles and repeats himself. This goes on for about two more times before my mother can finally gather herself . She steps in between them both and asks the doctor a question on her blood pressure. Ready to do anything to stop this volley of words between the Korean and the Mexican. This gets him talking about something he now understands and he now takes great care in explaining my grandma Lencha's medical condition to my mother.

My grandmother looks over at me with a confused look on her face and says "*Oye cabron*," now she's pissed, "*Me la van a pagar tu y tu mama cuando salganos de aquí.*" UH OH! I thought.

"*Solamente le hago una pregunta a este guey. Porque le dicen guey y nadie me quiere decir? Y tú y tu mamá creen que es un pinche chiste. Me la vas a pagar cabron.*"

I mistakenly started laughing again at this latest outburst from her. I also should have known better than to stand so close to her. As I try my best to stifle another round of laughter, knowing she's pissed and really means what she says, she quickly reaches over and grabs my ear lobe and twists it hard. I let out a harsh scream since my mouth is already open wide from laughing so much.

"AAAAYYOOWWWWW!" I yell out.

The doctor stops and looks over at us and looks startled as my mother turns to see what the commotion is all about. The nurse comes in just then. It must seem curious to her to see an angry old lady sitting on the bed holding my ear and twisting it. Now my abuela is cursing in Spanish while my mother tries to yank her grip off my ear. The doctor, not really understanding what the hell is going on, says something in Korean that NO ONE understands. The good doctor then tries to help my mother loosen the death grip on my ear. The nurse starts to laugh because it is quite a sight to see. My grandma Lencha finally lets go of my ear and now proceeds to yell at my mother.

"*Este chavalo domas sigue riye y riye. Mientras que tu y aquel GUEY siguen hable y hable.*" She goes on complaining wildly waving her hands in the air while I retreat to the corner of the room. I then check to see if my ear is still connected to my head.

Peace is finally restored quickly thereafter. My mother explains to the doctor about the similarity in his name with the Spanish cuss word. He actually got quite a kick out of the whole thing. He finished up the question and answer examination then set up some follow up tests for my grandmother. Luckily for me, the next trip to the doctor is scheduled for my father to drive them instead of me

Dr Wei told my grandmother he wanted her to quit drinking and smoking on that first visit. He made gestures in a motion of smoking a cigarette and drinking a bottle while waving a stern no with the other hand. "No more smoke and drink," he says. "NO MORE.

My grandmother looked at him quizzically. Then looked over at me and said in Spanish, "*Que dice este guey! Que esta loco o que?*"

"No grandma" I said, "dice que no debes fumar, ni tomar." Having known that she had some basic understanding of English phrases since I had heard her speak it before, she understood only too well what the doctor was telling her. She was just trying to claim ignorance over the whole thing.

"*Esta loco este Dr. Guey,*" she says as she makes a circular motion on the side of her head with her right hand and points at the doctor with her left. The doctor laughs and points at her and repeats his drinking and smoking gestures. For a minute there, the two look like little third graders in an elementary play making faces at each other.

We left Dr. Wei's office that afternoon with my mother promising Dr. Wei that, yes, she would do her best to get her to quit smoking and drinking. My mother sits in the back of the car with my grandmother and chastises her for being so disrespectful as we get into the car to go home.

*"Ay ama qué vergüenza,* él *es muy amable y no debes hacer así con* él*!"* she scolded my grandmother on the way home.

Grandma Lencha just took it all in stride waving my mother off with her hand, "*No, esta loco,*" she says.

I drove home not wanting any part of this argument between mother and daughter. This was between them. Besides, my ear was still sore from where she pulled on it before. I was still at her mercy. I was ripe for retaliation since I had to keep my eyes on the road while she was free to come at me from behind. The lingering pain in my ear kept my mouth shut. I'm not sure but I think I finally came to understand the meaning of the infamous "*jalon de mechas*" threat that lingered in the family for such a long time.

The second incident came as a result of the promise made to the doctor. A few days after the doctor's visit I received a call from my mother at home.

It was around six in the evening.

"Hello mama, como estas" I said.

She sighed into the phone which signaled a bad omen. "*Mira hijo*, I'm going to ask you to do something for me," she started. "Remember that the doctor said he doesn't want *tu abuela* to drink anymore? *Bueno, quiero que sepas* there's no more liquor at the house and she is out of cigarettes and I told Jose not to buy her anymore. He promised me he wouldn't even though *tu abuela* keeps threatening him," she said. "So if she calls and asks you to go get her something to drink and some cigarillos from the store, I want you to say no, *me entiendes*?" She tells me in a strong tone.

"Ugh, well, OK mama," I said, not really wanting to get into the middle of this. I had hopes of remaining neutral on this though I knew I probably wouldn't.

"I don't care if she threatens you. I don't want you buying her anything to drink or smoke. Do you understand me?" My mother repeated for emphasis.

"Sure mama, no problem. Don't worry about it," I said.

"Good, ok, *Aayy mijo*, how is my granddaughter? Good,.. *que bueno.* Then *entonces te dejo*, bye." I said goodbye and hung up the phone. I went back to watching TV. Ten minutes later the phone rang again.

"Hello," I said. "*Mijito, como estas*?" I knew I shouldn't have picked the phone up, dammit! It was my grandma Lencha's voice.

"*Hola ama*," I said. "*Bien gracias a dios y Usted?*" This was not good, I thought.

"*Bien gracias,*" she replied. "*¿Qué estás haciendo hijo mío? Tengo ganas de verte. ¿Por qué no vienen un rato para visitar*?"

She was asking to see the three of us. This was good. I thought if I had to go down over this, then I would not go down alone. I could throw myself on the floor begging for mercy from my mother, clinging to my child in my hands. My wife would have to fend for herself.

"*Pues, ah, es que, tengo la nina poca malita y este… tiene poca de calentura y ah,.. este,.. no se si podre sacarla hoy.*" My sentences were slow and unsure. I wondered if she had picked up on this. The phone was wet with sweat from my hands as I stood there waiting for grandma Lencha to respond. There was silence on the other end. I was desperately hoping she would fall for the line about my daughter having a slight fever.

"*Has estado hablando con tu mama verdad*," she asked me in a cold, almost chilling voice.

"Ah,..well, *este*, uhh..." I was busted. I didn't know what to say. I swear I could feel her cold hard stare coming at me through the phone line, piercing into my skull. I shuddered as I pondered my next move. I could try the sympathy approach first. "*Es que me dijo que si hablaba con usted que no fuera a comprarle nada, porque el Doctor no quiere que estés tomando, y fumando*" There it was, I had gone for the truth! If I was about to die then hopefully god was listening. He could give me a break and have mercy on my soul since I had told the truth. After all, if anyone knew how my grandmother could be, I figured it would have to be him, right?

" *Y so... este*… ah.." I was still stalling, waiting to see what her response would be. Would my daughter have to grow up without ever having known her father, I thought to myself.

Just then, she asked me in a stern voice. "*Y quién manda aquí, yo o tu mamá? ¿Quién es la mamá de tu mama*?"

She had a point. Technically my grandmother had priority to override my mother's authority if we were to follow the family chain of authority. I could always claim I had followed my grandmother's orders because she was the higher seeded authority figure. I was sure this argument could stand up to scrutiny in any court. Besides, a beer sounded good right about now.

"Uh… well, uh… *pues usted granma*," I said.

"BIEN DICHO!" She defiantly replied. *"Ahora, ve traime un seis de Budweiser y comprame un paquete de mis cigarrillos, ya sabes cuales,*" her mood was more upbeat now.

She sounded confident in knowing that her matriarch authority still stood firm. Her authority was not about to be breached. Actually what I thought I heard her saying to me was, "Don't worry about it. It's me. I can take care of your mother. You won't get into trouble. Besides, who should you be more worried about, me or your mother?" Maybe she hadn't said those exact words but I had been around her long enough to know how to read between the lines when she said one thing but meant something else.

"Ah, OK granma, *ahorita voy para ya,"* I said. I knew I would still be in trouble, but technically, not that bad. I feared my grandmother's wrath worse than I feared my mother's.

"*Y mijo traime esa niña preciosa para verla, tan Linda que está*," she said while asking to see her great grandchild.

She had validated the visit as being a family gathering in the event my mother asked what I was doing over at her house. I could always say she wanted to see her great grandchild, thus a trip to grandma's house would be required to meet this important obligation. The fact that she asked me to bring some beer and cigarettes to her was secondary to the matter. The more important issue here was that my grandmother wanted to see her descendant in the great family chain. I had a legitimate excuse in the event that my mother asked. I loaded up the family and headed for the liquor store. Ohh that abuela of mine, always thinking of everything.

# CHAPTER FOURTEEN

"Our next speaker is someone who is very near and dear to us all," said Victor. "He is someone who has worked partners with both the guest of honor and I and has been recognized for his heroic efforts time and time again." "He would like to say a few words on this auspicious occasion and so please help me in welcoming Raul Sotelo to the podium, Raul."

The audience started to applaud and I was surprised to see Raul here tonight so soon after his release from the hospital. Raul Sotelo and his brother Mario were two first rate officers. Both had joined the agency straight out of the military, solid performers whom you could count on to back you up in any situation. Over the years, the four of us, Victor, myself and the two Sotelo brothers had worked various fugitive details. We were successful in taking some of the baddest and most violent criminals off the streets. The brothers had thrived on the action. They were considered two of the best at what they did. While I had focused on moving up the chain, I had found myself doing more of the required duty behind a desk instead of out in the field. The brothers had remained on street duty where they thrived by feeding their craving for action.

"Naw bro, not me," Mario Sotelo used to say to me. "I'm happy for you if moving up the chain is what you want. But me and Raul are happier out here where the action is."

During our careers, there were times I wondered what would have been the more appropriate course of action to take. I had enjoyed my time in the field, chasing around after bad guys. Getting them off the street had been very gratifying work. But there comes a time when the income part of the job must be taken into consideration. Eventually you must pursue opportunities that provide you with financial security. More authority meant more responsibility. It also meant more money. With a growing family to support and the cost of living going up, there comes a time when each of us needs to make a decision for the future. I had chosen to take the required exams, putting in for supervisory job positions locally and out of town since your chances for selection were enhanced if you were willing to move somewhere. It showed you were willing to take what was offered. I didn't mind. This mindset had afforded me the opportunity to live in various places throughout the country and provided me a view of life outside the boundaries of El Paso. The job had taken me to various duty locations in the western part of the country. I had lived in Denver Colorado, Phoenix Arizona and had even spent time out west in California.

Victor and I kept in touch after he had taken the supervisory exam and passed it. He was still working in El Paso though. He had grown disillusioned with the hassles of the job, of which there were plenty, along with the scrutiny that comes from up above. Victor had put in for a transfer out of management and he accepted an assignment in the intelligence unit where he had been very happy. It required some travel, which freed him up from the drudgery that can be an everyday thing with a desk job. His second wife Bonnie appeared to have settled him down some and both seemed happy with his career move.

The Sotelo brothers though were another story. They both remained single, except for the time Raul had married that girl from the old barrio. She had gotten pregnant right after high school. He felt it was the right thing to do. Although a year later, it was clear that continuing the marriage would have resulted in one killing the other. Except for that brief one-year marriage, both brothers remained single and lived a life of work, party and sleep. Working out in the field meant staying out late, working odd hours and long days. The type of life that was not conducive to anyone trying to maintain a good family life anyway, proven time and time again by the number of agents that wound up on the divorce track as a result of this life. The Sotelo brothers thrived on it. As long as it made them happy and it was what they wanted, then so be it.

Funny, as teenagers we had all been from warring barrios that hated each other. I had grown up near barrio San Juan while the Sotelo's had been raised in the barrio known as El Segundo. The two barrios had been fighting each other for as far back as I could remember. We had all started together in the agency back in the early 80's and it was only after we had known and worked together for a few months that we found out where we had each grown up. We laughed it off since we had come to rely on each other so much. We had learned to depend on one another. There was never anyone else I felt safer with in the field than when I worked with Victor or the Sotelo brothers. Even Victor had grown up in the barrio known as Diablo and it was actually good to know that we had all been raised the way we had. Each of us knew the perils of the street. Our childhoods in the streets taught us to better understand the people on the other side. We grew up speaking their language. This made it easier for us to deal with the criminal element since we had all grown up knowing the life. The one they lived with but that we left a long time ago.

A couple of years ago, while I was still on my last tour in Arizona and while Victor was making a name for himself in Intelligence circles, the Sotelo brothers had been assigned to work fugitive operations. Their assignment was with a multi-unit task force that had infiltrated smuggling rings bringing tons of drugs into the country. Four months into the assignment, the operation would successfully lead to the prosecution of all the top operatives in the organization. The traffickers, unfortunately, had discovered the true identities of the undercover agents. When it came time for arrests to be made, there had been a shootout involving some of those agents. A gun battle had ensued at one of the warehouses in the airport district where the traffickers had set up shop. Several law enforcement agencies had responded. Four of the bad guys had been killed and two undercover agents had also died. One of them was Mario Sotelo. He had been a good person, someone very dependable with a good head on his shoulders. He knew right from wrong and he was one of those agents who genuinely believed in his work since as a child he had seen the evils that drugs brought upon the barrios.

There were times early in our career when we would sit around and talk about the old days. Those that we had grown up with and had fought with during the battle days of our youth. Each of us always seemed to respond in the same way when asked what had happened to members of the old crowd. Whatever happened to so and so?….Oh, man…he got a hold of some bad *caballo* and it killed him. Whatever happened to so and so?…naw, he did time for drugs. Last I heard he was a three time loser doing life. On and on it went with many of those we had grown up with listed as victims of the drug battles being waged in the barrios. Mario had come to believe that drugs were responsible for the decaying conditions in the old neighborhoods. He had joined the agency with a strong belief that he could make a difference. He was righteous in this belief. He knew he was doing the right thing and not just running out of the barrio and leaving those there to fend for themselves. He was giving back something positive by ridding the streets of el *caballo blanco and la maya*, street names for cocaine and Mexican brown heroin.

When he died, it was a blow to us all. Raul had taken his brother's death very hard. He was no longer the same after Mario died. Alcohol, with its power to dull the pain, became his best friend. He would miss work, spending days on end in a drinking binge, only to come back to work irritable, hung over and still feeling the pain of his loss. The higher ups tried to cut him a break but there was only so much they could cover. Inevitably there were suspensions for failure to report, confrontations with his superiors and other incidents. From what others told me, he had become a real pain in the ass to work with. His reputation and his desire were called into question as others became wary of working with him.

Finally, Victor and I sought him out a little over a year ago. We each vowed to help out our friend by removing him from this road of self-destruction. The road that could only lead to being fired or dead somewhere from the alcohol or a self-inflicted bullet. It took a long time and a lot of interventions. The three of us had deep discussions pierced by long periods of crying a few months before I was scheduled to retire. He finally committed himself to an alcohol rehabilitation center to dry out. The counseling combined with therapy seemed to be slowly bringing him back to the old Raul we used to know. When I transferred back home I made it a point to go see him a few times. Signs of progress were beginning to show. It was a struggle when he got out. We found out he had met someone while in rehab, a girl from the east side that turned out to be his savior. She too was struggling with the demons of the drink. But both had vowed to keep each other on the path to recovery and not fall back into the bottle's grasp.

I hadn't seen too much of him since he got out and I was surprised to see him here tonight. Apparently Victor had called him and asked if he wanted to come by to say something. He had agreed. Raul had always been a tall, rough looking guy. As he approached the podium, I could see he looked good. He embraced Victor in a bear hug and thanked him for the nice introduction. Victor sat down and Raul looked over my way as he began to speak.

"I'm not a person of very many words," he said as he returned his gaze to the assembled audience, "that was more my brother Mario's thing. He always loved to talk." The room grew silent since many in the crowd remembered and nodded their heads in affirmation. "But I just wanted to say a few words before this *cabron*...I mean, this guy leaves," he said.

The crowd erupted in laughter as Victor chimed in "No *ese*, you had it right the first time". Raul's face turned red as he grimaced and looked over at Victor who was laughing out loud.

He continued, "As most of you know, I have been going through some tough times since my brother passed away." He stroked his chin taking a moment to compose himself before he resumed. "My father always said that friendship is measured by those who are willing to stand with you in your darkest hour. There are those people that are always around you during the good times, but absent during the bad," he said. He pointed his index finger at me, "I am here to say that I'm glad that this man here is my friend," he looked at me and smiled. "This man never left me when I needed someone to be there, even though I thought I didn't need anyone." "This man knew the depth of my pain and helped me deal with it." As he spoke I was not sure I would be able to hold back the emotions on this one. Raul was getting misty eyed as he gripped the edges of the podium. "For this friendship and on behalf of my brother... I thank you and I wish you well."

The crowd broke into applause as he walked over to where I was sitting. I stood up and greeted him halfway while the entire row of people around us came to their feet. I embraced him in a traditional *abrazo*. It had been a long road for my good friend.

"You know he would have loved to have seen this day with you," whispered Raul into my ear.

"Yeah, I know," I said. "I miss him too."

The moment was very difficult for us both as we did our best to return from the emotion of longing for Mario's presence. He turned and walked back to his table with the applause from the gathered friends starting to wind down. I walked back to my seat with the pain of Mario's absence.

Sensing the need for a break from the emotional moment, Victor got up to the podium and announced it was now time for the slide show. Victor had put together a collection of photos of the many people I had been lucky to have worked with. Not everyone that wanted to could be here tonight to say their farewells. He had gotten a hold of quite a few though and some had agreed to send a farewell tape or send a message photo via the internet. He now wanted to show them to the assembled group. He fumbled with the connections trying to get the projector and the big screen set up behind the main table as the house lights went down. In the semi darkness, I thought about Raul and everything that had happened in his life.

The loss of a loved one is truly one of the most draining emotional experiences that we as human beings endure. Raul's situation got me to remembering the time we had to tell my grandmother my tia in San Francisco had passed on. My tia Josefina, the one who had been so much like her in many ways, had died of a stroke. Though these things are never easy, it was also bad timing since there were other family events going on at the time.

# CHAPTER FIFTEEN

It was around the late eighties. The time had finally come to move my grandmother out of the little house on Radford Street. The mortuary had made an offer on the house that my mother thought was fair. More importantly, she saw that the time had come to move her out of that neighborhood. Things had changed in the barrio known as La Roca. The two houses on the east side of my grandmother's house next to the tracks had been bought out and demolished a few years back. Now in their place stood a gated extension of the cemetery already filled up with grave markers. On my recent trips to see my grandmother, I would look out the side window and see family members of the deceased standing over the graves of their loved ones mourning and crying. It used to be that you could look out the window from the back door and see this sort of display a few yards back and away from the house. Now when you looked out the east side of the house, it was even closer and the only thing that separated the wall of the house from the row of graves was a chain link fence. This new section was right next to the house only a few feet away from the window. Imagine what it's like to look out a window and watch people grieve right outside your window. It was a depressing sight.

Meanwhile, the three houses on the west side were contemplating offers made to them, now that my grandmother's house was next to go. They knew it would only be a matter of time before they would be next. Many of the neighbors we had welcomed into her home and come to trust were no longer around. Kikirika, the friend of the family for as long as I could remember, had long left El Paso and now lived in Phoenix. El Gordo had passed away a few years ago. His love affair with the bottle had brought on cirrhosis of the liver and took his life at the age of fifty. Others like Chava, Pete and the Padilla family had left before. When they saw the writing on the wall they decided to leave. There were a couple of new families there now. There were people from Juarez who occupied the house where the Ruelas family used to live, across the street from my grandmother. They didn't talk to any of us, probably because they thought my grandmother was some sort of crazy woman, always telling them to keep their dog quiet. She would yell at them to keep it quiet whenever someone stopped by their house and honked the horn in front of the house instead of getting down to knock. My grandmother thought this was a rude method of behavior.

"¡*Bajense a tocar la puerta cabrones*!" she would yell. It wasn't like the old days anymore when it felt like a neighborhood with everyone watching out for each other. People from Juarez were getting their green cards and coming to live and work in El Paso even though they weren't supposed to. They were not trusting of us, their pocho neighbors, just as we were not trusting of them. That's just the way it always was between the *Mejicanos* and the *Mejicanos de alla.*

My mother saw how the barrio had changed.and decided to move her mother out to someplace closer to us. Though we weren't more than twenty minutes away from the old house, my mother decided on a smaller house on the other side of the freeway in the old Chelsea neighborhood. The new house was small but the neighborhood had once been a nice well-kept middle class suburb that was not as bad off as my grandmother's old neighborhood. Though it was on the down side now having seen its better days, the new house provided us with quicker access. She was only about five minutes away now, just on the other side of the freeway. My mother was able to put down a sizable payment with the money the mortuary had offered us on the old property. She even had enough to hire a woman to come stay with my grandmother and grandpa Joe.

It was apparent now even to me that my grandmother was getting old. She was closing in on eighty years of age . Grandpa Joe was starting to show the effects of what we would later learn was Alzheimer's disease. My mother, as usual, was entrusted with the immediate care of her mother. She too was getting up in her years and we were all glad she decided to hire someone to watch over them both. If my grandmother was looking old at eighty, my mother was now in her mid sixties and starting to show the strain of caring for two older people. She never complained about it. Sometimes though she would ask us for advice on some matters and on others she and my father would just decide to do it. Always with the two *viejitos* best interest at heart.

I was still working in El Paso, contemplating taking a transfer to Colorado. I would eventually take the job just to get out of El Paso to help me start a new life. Cities on the border with Mexico never really become boomtowns. They never prosper and always take a turn for the worse when things go bad south of the border. So I thought a change of scenery would do us good. El Paso was not the same town I had grown up in anymore.

People say you can never go home again. It was time for a change.

One day my mother called to ask if I could come over to her house. There was something she wanted to discuss with me. When I got there I saw she had been crying and was on the phone with someone from out of town since she kept asking what the flight schedules looked like.

*"Y el vuelo es direct a San José, verdad?"* she said into the phone.

My father, sitting on the side of the kitchen table as I walked in, gave me one of those not good news looks. I sat down with him and asked what was up. He told me my mother was almost off the phone. He would rather have her tell me.

She continued on the phone, "OK, *bueno entonces nos vemos, adios,*" she said and hung up the phone. She had a worried look on her face as she turned to look at me and I went over and hugged her.

*"Que tienes mama?"* I said. Tears welled up in her eyes racing down her cheeks as she looked at me.

I noticed that with age she was starting to grow smaller in size. Before she had held her own against my six feet two inch height. Now it seemed as if I towered over her as she appeared to me like an older Mexican woman growing short and chubby.

"*Murio tu* tia Josefina en San Francisco," she said. Her sister who had been so different from her, yet whom she had been so close to, had died the night before. I hugged her tight and didn't say anything to give her a chance to cry it out. She cried a bit, but in her usual take control of the situation approach, quickly stopped her weeping and looked at me.

"*Mira hijo*," she said, "I want to ask you a favor, could you fly out to San Jose with me and tu papa for the funeral?" We're not *chavalos* anymore and we could use your help driving around town" she said between tears.

"Of course mama" I said, "I would be happy to go with you and pay my respects to my tia."

"*Tambien, I want* you to do something else for me. I want you to go check on *tu abuela* tomorrow and see if she's OK. If she needs anything, buy it or get it for her, make sure they have enough food for the next few days, make sure everything is OK. I cannot go over there right now because she will know I have been crying and I'm not ready to tell her the news about Josefina just yet. I told Carolina the maid that we will be going out of town for a few days in an emergency but just check on her and make sure she's OK, OK *mijo*?" she said in a more composed tone.

"*Si* mama, no problem, I'll take care of it, don't worry," I promised.

The next night we flew out to San Jose California meeting up with my tia from Los Angeles and the rest of the family members living out west. Since the majority of the earlier clan from my grandmother's side had decided to move to California, there was a large contingency representing descendants from my grandmother's brothers and sisters. Some I knew, some I didn't. They were all glad to see my mother though as she introduced me to those in the family I didn't recognize. The older ones that were around my mother's age all got together. We hugged and cried. The *hermanos* stuck together talking about the old days while the younger *primos* my age hung around helping out as best we could and catching up on things.

I hadn't seen my LA cousins in awhile and we talked about the old days and the parties that my grandmother used to throw. How they all missed her California summer trips. She was getting too old to travel now and those long train trips were too tiring for her so she had stopped coming when she turned seventy-two. I caught them up on her latest antics. They laughed as they pictured her being as feisty and combative as ever.

We all acknowledged how for the rest of our lives, we would never again see a person like her. Each of us had benefited in some form or another from her wisdom and strength. I was glad to see that at least the cousins from my generation appreciated her for what she'd been to us and had brought to us. We were lucky to have her as a grandmother or an aunt. The stories of her survival had left a lasting impression on us all. Her "take no shit" attitude was ingrained in us all and I was impressed at how much of a far-reaching effect she had on the family. I was proud to know she was in El Paso. It was then that I realized more than ever, that we were fortunate enough to be the ones closest to her. She was a family treasure. Her care and safe being was in the hands of my mother. This made me feel proud since the feisty old woman had made quite an impression on the family and especially on me.

My thoughts then turned to concern though. I shared with my cousins the inevitable dread of having to return to El Paso and tell her about Josefina's death. My mother had decided to tell her upon our return since she was concerned, and rightfully so, that her heart might not withstand the shock of hearing the news. It was better to tell her after the funeral. We would do our best to let her know that everything had been taken care of. Her daughter had died peacefully and if we told her now, She would only worry about us being in California. Anxious and unable to be there, wondering how things were going. Besides, better to have my mother there by her side in the event she did get sick than for her to be out here in California too far away to care for her. I could tell the situation was tough on my mother too. I paid special attention to her making sure she was holding up.

The funeral was very traumatic and sad. We buried her on one of those bright sunny, cool days that Northern California is known for. We flew back to El Paso emotionally drained knowing there was one more difficult task ahead of us. I worried about my mother. How would she be able to handle telling her frail mother? On the plane ride back, I volunteered to go with her offering to help relay the news to my grandmother about my tia's death.

" *Ay mijo*, p*ues gracias, y también por ver ido con nosotros*," she said as she stroked my cheek with her hand. She looked tired sitting next to my father who had gone to sleep way before the plane was taxied for takeoff. I told my mother to try and get some sleep before we got back home. Normally she would say "I'll be fine, don't worry." This time she turned her head sideways and leaned back on the head rest of the plane seat. She fell fast asleep as soon as she closed her eyes.

I went back to my seat across the aisle from her. I tried to devise a way to tell my grandmother about her daughter's death in the gentlest way possible. There was none. As hard as I tried, I knew it would be the most difficult and emotional thing to do. I just hoped and prayed that the strain of hearing the news would not kill her. I looked over at my parents both fast asleep. I couldn't help but notice the lights on the horizon from the city of Phoenix below. It would be another hour before we landed. I wondered if my mother had a plan on how to do this because I sure didn't. I closed my eyes to the drone of the plane's engines that carried me into a far off deep sleep.

The next day I drove over to my mother's house in the afternoon to pick my parents up for the trip to my grandmother's. My mother slid into the front seat next to me while my father got into the rear. No one really said anything on the drive over. It was as if we all knew the dread of the approaching deed. It wasn't going to be an easy one. Five minutes later we arrived at my grandma Lencha's house. Carolina the nurse/maid was outside with my grandpa Joe standing in front of the house. She waved at us as I pulled up. I got out first and went around the car to help my mother step out of the car.

"Don't worry mama, we'll get through this," I said. She looked at me with a tense, tired expression on her face.

We walked towards the front door where grandpa Joe greeted me with a hug and led us into the house. My mother went in first with me a close second behind her. If she was to fall and needed someone to catch her, I wanted to be right behind her. My grandmother was sitting on the couch watching her afternoon TV novellas. She looked up at us as we walked into the house with that smile of hers. My mother did her best act to show nothing was wrong.

"*Buenas tardes ama*," she said to my grandma Lencha.

"*Buenas tardes hija*," she said, "*y a quien traes hay, chavalo cabron, ven aqui*".

Although I had been an agent working for the government, with a gun and badge, and not to mention I was also in my thirties, around her I felt like a young child. I had done my share of arrests, knockdowns and vehicle pursuits chasing bad guys, but there was still something that gave me the feeling of a little kid around this woman. I could not escape how she made me feel like her little man. Not in a "spoiled kid" kind of way since other than my older brother David, she never really spoiled anyone else. She didn't believe in spoiling children. She said it made them weak and left them vulnerable to a cruel world. So when she called me *chavalo cabron or cabroncito*, I knew she meant it with a lot of love and affection. It was her special way of greeting me.

When I was younger in my twenties, it bothered me since I felt she shouldn't greet me that way since I was no longer a little boy. But I came to realize this was her special greeting reserved for me over the years so I came to appreciate it with age.

"*Hola ama,*" I said and leaned over so she could plant a kiss on my cheek.

"*Como estas hijo mijo*?" she asked.

"*Bien ama, bien gracias a dios,*" I replied. That dangerous lump in my throat was again making its presence felt. I swallowed hard sitting next to my mother on the small sofa across from my grandmother. My father took a seat in a chair by the door while grandpa Joe stood in the doorway to take advantage of the slight breeze coming in.

No one spoke at first. My mother cleared her throat. My grandmother, I guess after having lived through so much and having understood people so well, suddenly changed the expression on her face. She went from happiness at seeing us to a look of concern.

"*Que pasa, Ana?" Que tienes*?" she asked my mother in a fearful tone.

The old lady was quick to spot trouble when it reared its ugly head. My mother cleared her throat, looked straight into her mother's eyes and said, "*Ama, tengo algo que decirte pero no quiero que te preocupes.*" My mother looked over at Carolina the nurse, "*Donde quedaron sus pastillas de alta presión*?"

Carolina quickly went into the kitchen to get my grandmother's blood pressure pills and she moved quickly to my mothers side as she knew what was to come. She left and returned with a glass of water to wash it down with.

*"Ama, murió Josefina en California. Le dio un ataque al corazón y por eso no estuve aquí estos* días, *fuimos a enterrarla*," said my mother in a barely audible tone.

She had tried to smooth it out as best as possible but had gotten to the point of the matter with the very first shot, which I thought was appropriate. Now we all stared and waited for my grandmother's reaction. She didn't say anything at first. She blinked a couple of times, looked down at the floor as if digesting the statement that just entered her brain but had not yet reached her emotional button. She blinked again and tightly closed her eyes. Her lips began to tremble and she gripped the armrest on both sides of the recliner chair. Her eyes closed tighter and tighter. You could see the pain was coming at her from all angles. She reached for her heart which caused us anxiety. My mother quickly jumped over to her, asking how she felt.

*"Ama, estas bien?"* she said as she wrapped her arms around her mother.

Just as she said this, my grandmother let out a yell that came from the very depths of her soul. She moaned out loud. The tears started coming out as she wailed a cry, piercing into the deepest reaches of my being. I felt like yelling out and begging God to relieve her of this pain but I knew that she had to let it go. My mother, quickly thinking on her feet, called for Carolina to give her the pill.

"*Damela ya*! She ordered. Carolina jumped to her feet and rushed to my mother's side. She took the pill and placed it hard into my grandmother's mouth. She grabbed the glass of water and poured it into her mouth between cries.

"¡PERO CÓMO! *¿Cómo puede ser que murió mi hija?* she demanded. "*Dios Mio, como puedes permitir esto*," she cried.

My mother called to me and I stood next to my abuela as she clung on to me with a grip that dug into my arm. My mother held her on one side while I held her on the other, moving her close as she wailed up to the sky searching for an answer from God.

"*Porque dios mio porque*?" she cried.

My mother kept asking her how she was feeling. It was obvious that even she felt the pain and once again, her concern now was how my abuelas physical condition would hold up. Everyone in the room tried to keep their own emotions in check, but it was too hard. My father, who tried to console my grandmother, got up and walked away when the anguish in her cries was too much for him to bear. My grandpa Jose stared out the screen door, not really looking at anything, but caught up in his own emotions. He had always liked my tia Josefina. He thought of her as a young Lencha. I knew he was thinking how hard it was going to be to let her go.

My mother continued checking my abuelas physical condition. She answered my grandmother's questions as best as she could. When did she die? How did it happen? Why didn't you tell me the day she died?

"*Porque iba ser mucho para ti*!' she said and as tears rolled down her face.

She knew her mother would not approve but she had been right. It would have been too much for the old woman to bear. My mother understood the importance of doing her duty. Going out to California to represent my grandmother. Grandma Lencha couldn't attend, for in her older frail condition, the strain would have been too much for her. The flight and the trauma of the funeral might have killed her.

"*Se que te ibas a poner mala, por eso no te dije,*" she cried.

My grandmother buried her head in my shirt and cried as I had never seen her cry before. She held onto my arm and I hugged her as I rocked her head back and forth. I kept telling her not to cry anymore.

"*Ya ama, ya no llores, te vas a poner mala*, sshhh," I said to her as I stroked her gray hair. She held me in her grip. I could feel it loosening on my shirt as her cries started to become little whimpers. Now was the time we really had to watch her. She was either coming to grips with it or her body was spinning out of control, ready to collapse.

"¿*Estás bien ama, estás bien*?" I asked.

I thought of pulling her head back to check to see if her eyes were rolled back. I was afraid we were going to lose her but she shook her head up and down in reply to my question. She was gradually coming back to reality.

"Si," she said, "estoy bien mijo," she replied as she patted me on the side of my soaked shirt with her hand.

She was emotionally spent from the momentary burst of crying. The fact that another of her children was gone was now setting in. She was coming to grips with the news. My mother quickly started barking out directions to each of us. We quickly all jumped into action.

"Bring me her sleeping pills," she yelled at Carolina. "Pick her up and carry her to the bed!" she ordered pointing at me.

"Find me the doctor's phone number" she ordered my father. She was an expert at caring for her mother and knew exactly what was needed. I picked up my grandmother's fragile little body and carried her into the bedroom where I placed her down on the bed. My mother brought in the glass of water and told me to step outside for a minute.

She wanted to be alone with her mother to reassure her everything would be alright. There was a bond between the two women that years of emotional turmoil had nurtured between them. Though I was a special part of both, the two of them were all that mattered now. No one could understand or come between the closeness they shared. A closeness that had gotten them through all these years. I respected this moment of peace between them and got up to leave the room. Before I closed the door, I looked behind and saw my mother give my grandmother an embrace, holding her like a little child holds her favorite doll. The moment between the two needed no words. She's going to make it I thought, my mother would see to it. They hugged each other tightly in silence. I slipped out quietly, gently closing the door behind me.

The experience of having seen mother and daughter bond made me understand the meaning of strength and compassion. Their commitment to each other amazed me while at the same time provided me with a humbling experience. Up to that point, I had not understood the uneasy relationship between the two when it came to me. It was not until that day my mother had opened my eyes by recounting the story about the death of her brother.

At first I failed to understand it because I had been too absorbed in my own selfishness. My grandmother had always held on to me so tightly. Yet I felt my mother was condescending in her reactions towards this. My failure was in not understanding that there was more to their relationship than just me. I was so caught up in finding the reason for their attitude towards me that I couldn't see I was but part of a larger, more important picture, one that held the answer. The motivation factor in their relationship was the countless sacrifices they had gone through together.

My grandmother had stood up for her child when threatened by her father long ago. She had made a choice to do the right thing. She left her marriage for the sake of my mother and her siblings at the expense of her husband. My mother had never forgotten that sacrifice. Through the hard times right after the depression, my mother had been forced to shed her childhood years to work and provide for her mother. She had helped raise her siblings to insure the family would survive.

In the sixties, a woman raising five kids by herself was perceived as a scandal. I cannot begin to imagine what it must have been like to go through it in the late 1930's and 1940's. Together they had pulled each other through the toughest of times. Each armed only with their will and a promise that they would see it through no matter what.

Long ago, my mother had told me how they had made this pact with each other. One of the few times my mother spoke to me about the events in her past. They realized that in order to make it they were going to have to rely on each other. This was not the stuff of typical Mexican American families. It goes without saying that times were hard. Knowing especially how we *Mejicanos* can be critical towards our own. Yet even this they endured. They clung to each other and persevered. They had survived through sheer determination. I thought of this as now both stared death in the face.

They needed no one else except each other at that very moment. I came to believe my mother had realized another sobering thought that night. Soon she would face this challenge alone. It was apparent my grandmother's health was becoming a factor. Death would soon steal her from their bond leaving my mother to fend for herself.

There were times I found myself going back to that day, drawing from its ideals. Now more than ever I was grateful to be extracting the lesson both women worked hard to teach me. The main objective was to carry on.

"*Dios no te da más que lo que puedas sostener*" my mother would always say. Over the years I learned she was right, God never gave you more than you could handle.

I had planned to stop by and check on my abuela to see if she was OK a few days later. First though I checked on my mother the day after it occurred and she seemed fine. Worn out but fine. I told her of my intent to go see Grandma Lencha in a couple of days. She agreed and told me she just needed some time to herself now. She would need time to take in the events of my tia's death and deal with it in her own way. I agreed, if anyone knew what was right for the woman, it was my mother. A few days later I stopped by the house off of Chelsea Street. It was close to dusk. One of those cool March nights in the desert when the grip of winter starts to give way to blustery spring winds.

I walked into the little house. Grandma Lencha was in the kitchen, sitting at the table fussing over a box of small gardenias that Carolina had bought for her at the flower shop down the street. Soon they would be ready for planting. Abuela seemed absorbed in her work. Preparing the small plants for planting in the flower boxes located in front of the house. Her duties consisted of gently pulling on the stems to insure they had strong roots. This was crucial in having healthy plants. Carefully she cleaned off the little pilings of dirt from the petals and arranged them in the order they would be planted the next day.

She was humming a song, an old Mexican bolero song from the past that I had heard her sing before. I found this curious in light of the events of the last few days. Either she was dealing with my tia's death with a much better attitude than expected or she was drugged up and feeling no pain from the pills Dr. Wei had prescribed. I hoped it was a combination of both.

She looked up and smiled as I approached her. I hung my coat over the chair across from her. I pulled it out before I caught myself and realized I had forgotten something. Quickly, I went over to kiss her on the forehead as a form of greeting.

"*Como estas mi amor*?" she said. "Look at the pretty flowers Carolina brought for planting." She kept fussing and talking to them like babies lying in their cribs.

Over the years her command of the English language had gotten better. Lately, she would speak to me in English more often, especially when it was just the two of us. She told me she enjoyed speaking it since it gave her a chance to practice in helping her become more proficient.

"*Si ama*, they're very nice," I said, "Looks like they should bloom just in time after the spring plantings."

My eyes scanned her face. I tried to tell whether it was the drugs or her natural mood keeping her in this pleasant, comfortable state. I tried to read her without letting her know what I was doing. As always, she was better at reading a person than they were at reading her.

"I guess you are wondering if this old *vieja is bajo la droga* or if it's really me today eh?" she replied. I quickly turned, pretending not to understand what she was talking about.

"*No ama, porque dices eso*?" I said.

"In *Englich* por favor" she commanded.

Man, I thought! She must really be in the mood to practice her English.

"No grandma," I said. "Why would you think that?" I responded as I crossed my leg, one over the other.

She went back to coddling her box of baby plants and reached for the spray bottle on the table full of water.

"Because you have a habit of crossing your legs like that when you lie *cabron*" she said. She continued watering her plants as a coy smile began to form over her mouth.

I had never noticed this giveaway behavior of mine. Knowing her keen sense at watching people's mannerisms, I had nothing to come back with. I just smiled when I realized I was busted.

"Well, no *ama*, you know I just...just wondered how you were doing from the other day but you seem to be doing OK with everything *verdad*. I mean, considering..."

I was still not sure how to approach the topic. Whether to just get to it or skate around it as best I could. Knowing my relationship with her over the years, I was sure she would want me to get straight to the point.

So I continued, "How are you feeling? You look better than the other day," I said as I arched my eyebrows up and gave her a curious look.

I had hoped to slide into it gently by focusing on the positive side of her demeanor tonight. She continued to arrange her plants in an organized manner, moving one ahead of the other, occasionally spraying some with water while she let out a deep, long sigh pondering my question. Her eyes projected a far off glance. In her mind she revisited the site of her pain but oddly enough her facial expression seemed to be one of acceptance. A look of someone who once again comes to grips with the hardships of life.

"¡Pues *qué más hace uno*!" she replied..

"IN ENGLISH, PLEASE, ENGLISH THANK YOU!" I said jokingly as I mimicked her command from before.

This startled her back to my presence and after shooting stern looks at me from the surprise, we both laughed and broke the discomfort of the moment.

"*Yes mijo*, I know you are right. Speak English, yes," she said and returned to humming the bolero song..

She was in a comfort zone of sorts. I found this to be one of the amazing things about her character. Throughout my entire life, I always tried to understand what made her tick, where she drew her strength from, what she was made of, how she handled crises in her life. What was it that made her come back from them? What gave her the strength to deal with the problems life handed you.

I don't know how others view elders in their own family. I understand there are different cultural levels of respect and admiration and I can speak only of my own heritage as a *Mejicano* since as Hispanics we are taught the importance of our elders. At least I was. As a child I was taught to honor and respect my elders. They were revered for their position within the hierarchy of the family and respected for their wisdom. They were a part of your past. They were full of wisdom, foresight and experience. They were respected simply because they had succeeded in living a long life. Their age was their testimony at surviving everything in their life.

To me, my grandmother was one of the most fascinating people I ever met. Here was a woman born in the early part of the century. Someone who survived and had become part of the great exodus from Mexico spawned by a revolution. A woman who had contributed to the construction of this most powerful country. By the time she was nineteen, she had experienced more than someone twice her age. A person who learned so much about life armed with a knowledge that did not come from life's benefits but rather from its pitfalls.

I had seen this woman exhibit the level of *aguante* that my grandpa Joe had talked about. The meaning of which I hadn't understood until I came to see all she had gone through. This was the mean woman who had scolded me all those years ago, left me in the back yard and forced me to deal with the ghosts of the cemetery. This was also the same woman who held me in her arms with the most tender of embraces I have ever known. I was there to see her play cards with the men and drink from the bottles of tequila as they did. In the mornings I would awaken and look out the bedroom window and still see her sitting there. She would be playing cards with the last surviving member with enough *aguante* to still be awake. The others passed out from a hard night of drinking or sleeping on the patio floor next to her. She then had the stamina to get up from an all night poker game, go to the kitchen and prepare a breakfast feast for everyone.

All this she did with nothing more than two cups of black coffee to keep herself going. A woman who never attended academic school yet forced herself to learn how to read and write by sitting with me or my sisters while we did our homework. We taught her about history, we taught her to multiply and discussed world events with her. She was an eager student who absorbed her material like a sponge.

A woman, who endured a childhood of struggle, survived two husbands and married a third who all adored her for the woman she was. A woman with a mean streak that could scare the H out of Jesus Christ yet sit there and pamper her grandchildren and make you feel you were her one true blessing in life.

I sat across the table from her, now in my late thirties, older, hopefully wiser and more educated yet I still found this small Mexican woman with the wrinkled face and graying hair to be one of the most fascinating people in my life. Wrapped in this five foot three inch frame was a person that dealt with adversity far better than most.

How had she accomplished this? What was the secret to her durability? There had to be a potion, I thought, a pill or a secret formula! What was this ability that enabled her to deal with it all? The key was not stashed away in a vault but in the mind of this little old brown woman, humming a song from the past, stroking the leaves of her plants, caressing them as if holding a baby's behind.

"*Ama*, how do you do it?" I finally asked. "How do you deal with something like this and keep from going insane?" I blurted out.

She stared at me with a quizzical look on her face. "*Que quiere decir INSEN, qué es eso*?" she asked

"*Es cuando uno se vuelve loco por lo que pasa*," I explained. "*Como aguarda usted la pacencia de no volverse loco en esta vida*?" I demanded.

A smile crossed her face. She noticed the desperation on my face and must have felt pity for me. She could sense the hunger in my words as I searched for the miracle answer to the question. She stopped tending her flowers and placed the water bottle on the table.

"*Hijo mio*, what would you expect me to do?" She wrapped her hand in a fist and placed it on her chest.

"*Si*, Josefina's death was a great blow to me. It took me back to the horrible empty feeling I had when Antonio died. Losing one child is a most difficult thing to go through but losing two in your lifetime, *aayy*, there are no words to describe it."

She sat back in her chair, made the sign of the cross over her chest and said something in a soft tone. She stared out the window at the night sky so clear and full of stars.

She returned her gaze to me, "*Pero en esta vida mijo*, you cannot choose when pain will enter your life. There will be times when sorrow and pain will make you want to rip your chest open like this," she said as she gestured, showing her chest open reaching for her heart, "and pull out your *corazon* just to stop it from hurting."

"Pain is part of la *vida*. You cannot have happiness without having sorrow. Not understanding pain is to allow it to destroy you, to understand it is to accept that it makes you stronger." She said as if speaking about a long time acquaintance.

She pushed back from the table and rose from her chair. She walked over to the counter top where she had placed a photo of my tia Josefina and her. In the photo, my tia was in her twenties and Lencha was in her forties. The picture was taken in Las Vegas and both stood in front of one of those huge slot machines, about eight feet high with a monster handle attached to it that you have to pull on after placing a dollar bet. They had hit a jackpot on it worth a thousand dollars. Both stood proudly in front of the machine. The photograph caught the very essence of the two women. Both drank hard liquor, smoked and loved to gamble. They went to Vegas after my abuelas period of mourning as a widow from her second marriage.

Their pose said as much about their attitude as it did about their similar features. In the photo, they looked like two fighters standing over a conquered opponent, droopy eyes reflecting a hard night of drinking and gambling. Daring the world to criticize them for being independent.

Both had experienced ups and downs with men. Both found them to be more hassle than what they were worth and both were now independent of them. They were proud of the fact each had proved capable of taking care of themselves and their offspring.

They were smiling, arms around each other in triumph with a camel cigarette in my tia's hand, my grandmother holding a rum and coke in hers. She stared at the photo for a few seconds, reminiscing about the emotions of that night in the photo and said in a soft tone, "And you have to know mijo, that life, as it always proves to be, is very unfair. There will be times when life's pains will wrap you in its shadow and choke you until you think you will burst," she said as she returned the photo back to the spot on the counter. "But God never gives you more than you can handle. *Diosito no te da mas que puedas aguantar*," she said.

I smiled as I remembered my mothers saying the same thing. Now I know its source. She turned and walked back to her seat at the table as she kept talking.

"You will never know when or how much pain will come to your life." She sighed and sat down while crossing her hands in front of her, in the same manner as her daughter. "You must accept that life is a journey filled with anger and laughter, joy and sorrow and pain and happiness."

Her dark brown eyes stared straight at me, still appearing like two pools glistening against a full moon though looking worn and tired. They stood out now as they had back in her younger days and it reminded me of the beautiful woman she had once been.

"I look back now, mijo, and see I have lived a long life with much pain. But believe me when I say that God has been merciful to me for I have lived long enough to be here today."

I looked at her in a curious way as to question why she would say that after what she had just been through.

" Yes," she said, "I know the pain of losing two children. I have known the pain of hunger in my stomach. I have done things I was not proud of just to survive. But God has given me the strength to come through it all. He has blessed me with people who love me and helped me survive. *Asi como tu mama,*" she said.

I smiled at her. It was good to hear her acknowledge all that my mother had done for her.

"Your mama was always there for me. That is why I love you so much because you are a part of her. I know God has blessed me because he let me live this long to sit here and see my *nieto* grow up and be a good man," she said, as she wrapped her worn wrinkled hands over mine. I reached over to kiss her forehead again.

"If there is one thing an old *vieja* like me can teach you, *hijo mio*, is to be at peace with yourself. Find a peace within you and when you do, everything that happens in life will be easier to deal with. *Ahorita*, you are in the middle of your life's journey. I am coming to the end of mine. Before I die I wish to share with you this secret to a long life." She paused momentarily while my grandpa Joe walked by her and placed his hand on her shoulder as a show of support. She squeezed his hand and he walked on into the bedroom. No words were exchanged but each knew what the other was saying by their touch.

"Some things in life you can control… who you marry, how you make a living, where you live. These things are within your power, " she said. "But everything else is in God's hands. Accept this in your heart knowing he will help you survive. I can only hope you live a long life, but I will not be here to find out. So always remember the one thing that will keep you, como dice, from losing your *INSANITEE,* " she tried hard to pronounce the new word for the day correctly, "and that is *siempre*, always be at peace within yourself. Always try to be a good person. Take the bad and know it will not be forever. Take the good and be thankful, for it too will not last forever. Be humble in your thoughts but never let others take advantage of you. You are no better than anyone else but no one else is better than you. Be kind to those who are true and reject those who are not. Fight for what you know is true and be a good man. Find your inner peace by knowing who you are and stay true to that person. Believe in this because it will be the source of your strength. This is my belief that I give unto you because this is what helped me survive." she placed her hands over mine again in the same way as my mother.

" I do not know what life will bring you or where you will be when you are old and gray like me. But you are blood of my blood and remember if I survived to this old age happy and wiser then so will you. *Querido hijo*, I never doubted you. You are the son of my oldest daughter who was my greatest strength. Remember us both when you need to draw strength. We will be there for you as my mother was for me and your mother was for you. You will find us in your peace, we will be there for you always for the rest of your life". And with that the mother of my mother, the matriarch of the clan, the center of the family universe to whom we all paid homage, passed on all which she had gathered from a lifetime of trials and tribulations to the next link in the family chain.

The bond of courage and determination that evolved from my mother and grandmother would be water in the well from which I would draw strength and comfort. Their legacy would be an example of perseverance through their combined efforts. I would rely on their wisdom when faced with those difficulties in life that would surely come to pass. It is the one ingredient of my character that still pays tribute to them by way of its longevity. A fact that resonates within me.

It was getting late and grandma Lencha was looking even more tired now so I thought it best to leave and let her get some sleep. I could tell she wanted to talk more, Carolina the caretaker and the one outsider who had come into the family in these last few days had shown me she truly cared for the two *viejitos*. She came in and placed a sleeping pill on the table before her next to a glass of water. Lately Carolina had gotten into this stubborn habit of standing there waiting for her patient to take the prescribed pill at the prescribed time. This irritated my abuela to no end.

I was family and Carolina would never think of asking me to leave. She was very punctual when it came to my grandmother taking her medicines on time. My mother had seen to that and would not tolerate anything less since now she was the one who hired and fired. My mother had now taken control of all her mothers' business matters along with her personal dealings. Carolina knew I spoke for my mother and was aware of the power I knew my mother held over her. But her attitude towards my abuela was fine with me since it was this stick to the schedule behavior that made me realize she truly cared for the old couple so I thought it best to leave.

"*Bueno ama ya me voy*," I said to her as she looked over at Carolina who stood there waiting for her to take the pill.

Carolina had been with them for the last year and a half. She was up to speed on my grandmother's tricks at not taking medication when she was supposed to. At one time, pills were winding up in trash cans or being flushed down toilets when all the time, my abuela claimed she had taken them. When my mother found out, there had been hell to pay. Both granma Lencha and Carolina had gotten a tongue lashing from my mother on the importance of taking her medication. Carolina had been threatened with the loss of her job. So now the caretaker made sure that the sneaky *viejita* took her pills at the prescribed time and in her presence as commanded by my mother.

"*No te vayas mijo, quédate y platicamos más,*" she said.

"*No, ya me voy*, I have to work early tomorrow morning *ama* but I'll try and come back next week, OK?" I said.

She nodded her head disappointingly and gave Carolina a dirty look blaming her as the reason for my leaving. Carolina would have none of that. "*Andele tomese su pastilla, senora,*" Carolina pleaded.

"*Si andele, tomasela o después no vengo,*" I joined in trying to help get my grandmother to take the pill. Carolina shot me a thank you smile since we both knew how difficult abuela could be. Seeing as how she was outnumbered she picked up the pill, threw it into her mouth and washed it down with the water. I kissed her on the forehead and heard her say "*par de cabrones*' ' or something like that although I acted as if I didn't hear it. I walked out the door leaving Carolina to argue with her about putting on her nightgown before the effects of the pill kick in.

# CHAPTER SIXTEEN

Summers in Arizona can be a brutal time. Though Tucson and El Paso share the common distinction of being desert cities, one is located in the Sonoran desert (Tucson) which is considered a live desert where more plant life thrives in the heat. Whereas the other one (El Paso) is located in the more dormant Chihuahua desert where plant life is less in abundance and thus gives the desert a bleaker appearance. Both have a natural beauty to them, which only we as desert rats can come to appreciate.

The wide open views go on forever and seem endless as the deserts go on and on. For hundreds of miles around the only sight on the horizon are the mountain ranges that punctuate the sky. The extreme heat is the common factor shared by both desert cities. In regards to which is hotter, I think Arizona exceeds Texas in this category simply because of its proximity to the well known Death Valley, Palm Springs and Desert Springs areas where it's really hot.

Since I was born into this climate I did not mind it. I actually found it to be a welcome relief for me after having spent three years in the bitter cold winters of Colorado. Though I did view Colorado as one of the most beautiful states in the country, I was a desert rat, more used to the heat and the desolation that the desert exhibits in its own beautiful way. CORRECTED UP TO THIS POINT

I left the cold of Denver winters for the heat of the Tucson summers with no regrets. It felt good to be back in my element. I was used to spending summer days indoors until late afternoons. Then you could go grab a cold beer and sit outside to watch the sun go down over the mountain range. It had been five years since I left El Paso. Though I did make periodic visits back as required to see the family on holidays or special occasions, my work and the high cost to travel from Colorado to Texas kept me from the closeness of my mother and grandmother.

Life had moved on and my family and I enjoyed life in other parts of the country besides El Paso. In fact, truth be known, I did not miss the town at all. Except for family members and the food and a few close friends, there was nothing I really missed about the old hometown.

Denver had somewhat of a Hispanic culture atmosphere which, as is typical in towns located away from the border, consisted of two main Latino groups. The first was, Hispanos raised in the U.S. but with no ability to speak Spanish. They did understand or practice Mejicano traditions except for what their grandparents told them. Half the time they couldn't understand since their elders didn't speak English which created a communications gap.

The second group consisted of the illegals who had made it as far as the interior cities looking for work. Finding jobs that the local populations, which included the Anglo and U.S. born Hispanics, along with most every other cultural race found to be beneath them or were unwilling to work.. These were the jobs they knew would not pay enough to put bread and butter on the table. These were also the jobs the immigrants considered the American dream.

Tucson on the other hand provided more of a cultural blend between the local American born Mejicanos and the *recently* arrived from across the border Mejicanos that I was used to. There was a connection to the families in the old country that existed between them and the US Hispanos and here in Tucson it was more evident than in Colorado.

There was always someone who had family members in Mexico and traveled freely back and forth across the border to maintain a connection to the old ways. Gradually, family members brought them back to America and helped them understand US culture by assimilating them into the Chicano or Hispano or Latino bred society they followed, depending on the family creed and beliefs. Close proximity to the border was also a factor and more of what we were used to being from a town like El Paso. Tucson just seemed more appealing and more comfortable. Besides, El Paso was only a four-hour drive compared to the twelve long hours it took to go from Denver to El Chuco.

We had not made this drive south on I-25 until the second year there in Denver when my mother called to tell me Grandpa Joe had died. He had succumbed to Alzheimer's quickly over a one-year period. It had robbed him of his individuality and caused him to slowly wither away. Although he had not been true blood to me I had come to love the man as my true grandfather. A part of me was glad not to have been around for the slow deterioration of his mind and spirit.

I know this was not a kind thing to say but I knew him as he was and I wanted to retain this image I had of him laughing and singing and dancing *corridas* and *rancheritas* with my grandmother at family parties. This was how I wanted to remember him. He had the calmest demeanor of any one person I had ever come to know. When he drank, he did not become violent or sarcastic but rather he would change into this carefree person with a zest for life who expressed his enjoyment through dance. He had been a great competition dancer before he ever started his career working with trains. My grandmother's stories told of how he had been impressed with his charm but she also went on about how he did a mean tango. Since grandma Lencha had been a party person, it stands to reason she must have been impressed with his abilities on the dance floor. She told me once of his mastery of the difficult dance moves one must perform when dancing traditional *rancheras estilo Norteño.*

In the days during the family Christmas parties at the old house, he was so good that he would tire my grandmother out and grab one of my sisters as his dance partner. My older sisters, Americanized by habit and being more up to date with the latest dance moves by the Supremes than with the ranchera dance moves of La India Maria would always hide somewhere outside the house or laid claim to just recently having sprained an ankle to avoid having to dance with him. It wasn't necessarily that they didn't like dancing with him but more of the fact he was just too good of a dancer to keep up with. He demanded perfection and he wanted you to move on his timing and perform intricate moves, which was revered in Mexico but far too sophisticated for a family Christmas party in barrio La Roca. He would dance in the traditional way of Ranchera, which involved complicated moves by design. Still, he was a good man, fun to be around and impressive to watch as he amazed us with his footwork.

He was gone now and so we drove the long way home to Texas to be there to bury him in the cemetery located behind the old house on Radford Street. The house of course was no longer there. It had been torn down soon after its sale. The land was now part of the extended burial area now referred to by the mortuary office as the southern plots. The entire small block of homes on Radford Street had been leveled. The area where the old street was located, where we had played so many street games of kickball and football and which had been the battleground for many street fights was now gone. There was nothing there of note to remind anyone it had once been a neighborhood.

As we stood by the grave plot listening to the priest conduct his mass hymn in prayer to the saints above to take this old man into their fold, I could not help but stare at the area and remember what it had once been. More than once I noticed my mother also stare over at the old location no doubt wondering the same thing. She sat next to my grandmother throughout the rosary the night before and again today at the burial and as she leaned over closer to my grandmother.

I saw her whisper something while she glanced a look at the old location. My grandmother, now older and appearing much smaller and weaker to me, looked over at the cemetery plots sitting atop the old homestead smiling with reminiscence as she nodded in agreement to my mothers whispers. Once again they were together at their time of loss. Once again I could not help to remember the closeness to each other in their time of need. Apart they were saddled with their grief over yet another loss but when they came together, one fed off the other to provide a comfort zone. In their state of sorrow, you could see the comfort each provided the other. But of more concern at the time was the way they had both aged in the short time I had been gone.

After the funeral and at the end of our solemn goodbyes, I had returned to Denver determined to try and keep in touch more by phone or take more return trips to check on them in person. The demands of the job and the hassles of everyday life never did allow this to happen as often as I'd wished. My subsequent request to the agency for a transfer to Arizona had in fact been pursued partly as a result of my desire to be closer to them.

The move to Tucson had been good for us. So on this warm Friday summer night while my wife and I sat outside watching the stars, talking about the day's events and my daughter's latest episode in school, the phone rang and I rushed inside to pick it up. "Hello…hi mama, *que milagro!*" I said into the phone though she did not respond.

Anytime she called, I would always say it was a miracle since we didn't talk as often as we'd like and she would always jokingly reply "*Si verdad!*"

Except that tonight there was no reply. There was something wrong and the dread that creeps into a person's mind right before someone gives you bad news begins to enter your body and soul.

"What's wrong mama?" I said. "Tell me".

She wouldn't say anything but I heard her sniffling on the other end. This was not good. Finally a response, " I think you better come home mijo, it's your grandma," her voice reflected a sadness that I had never heard before similar to that of a small child after a futile cry when no more tears can be forced out.

"I don't want you to speed down here but try and get here as soon as possible, it's her heart and the doctor says she may not make it." I held a phone in my hand but I could not tell where this voice in my head was coming from.

For a split second, this is all I could remember about that moment. My mind had somehow frozen and kept repeating each word I heard with emphasis on the three words *not make it!*. I tried to gather my thoughts as quickly as possible

"Sure mama, don't worry I'll be there by midnight or so," I said.

"Hurry" she replied and hung up. It is an amazing thing when you stop and think about it. How the measurement of time can sometimes go by in the blink of an eye or on a moment's notice stop dead in its tracks and drag on for what seems like an eternity. No matter how hard I tried while I was trying to grab what I needed, make sure I had everything locked up, make the necessary phone calls, and gas up the car. I was trying to get all the little things that need to be accomplished done, while trying to maintain control over my emotions. Time could not go by fast enough to satisfy me.

You function in a most excruciating state of tension when your mind wants the next few hours to be over with so you can physically be where your mind already is. In your mind you are there but trying to get your body to catch up with your mind can be agonizing. Almost like an out of body experience, your body trying to catch up with your mind.

Around 1:30 in the morning, we arrived at Providence Hospital located on the west side of the city where the rest of the family had already assembled. Not everyone was there since some had come in shifts. Others were out of town on route back or some had still not been found to advise them of the news.

I got stopped in New Mexico for speeding by the State Police and I shoved the ticket deep into my pants pocket as I walked in and saw my mother talking with my uncle, both in deep discussion off to the side of the hallway. The door leading into the emergency waiting room was filled with my sisters, brother in laws, nieces, nephews and various assorted family members and friends.

It was a Friday night and it was the weekend. The hospital was filled with members of other families waiting for the gunshot victims, the stabbing and family feud patients who were no doubt laying on beds in the various treatment rooms down the hall just beyond the double doors with the bold letters across it that said "NO ADMITTANCE."

I said a few polite hellos to some of my family members and soon my mother, having left my uncle pondering her latest recommendation no doubt, moved over to greet me by way of a hug and a kiss. She looked stressed and tired but managed to feign me a smile to let me know she was glad to see me.

"Hi mijo, did you get a ticket?" she asked in a worried tone.

"No, it's fine mama no problems on the road" I thought it best not to tell her about the sudden stop in New Mexico.

"Where is she?" I asked.

My mother replied by telling me that she was still in ICU emergency. She recounted the events of the night and told me granma Lencha had collapsed at home. Carolina had called my mother in a panicked state. My mother being the leader that she is, immediately shot into her "take control of the situation" mode and directed my father to call the ambulance and give them the address to the house while she got hold of Dr Wei.

They then both jumped into the car and drove over to her house just as the ambulance was pulling into the driveway. As my mother rushed into the house, she could tell her mother was having trouble breathing even with the help of the oxygen mask which she now used everyday to help her breath. My mother had removed her mask long enough for her to tell her my mother in her exhaustive state that she didn't know if she was going to pull through from this one.

While my mother was relaying this story to me, she began to cry and I held her close and told her not to worry so much, that the woman was going to outlive us all. Fortunately, the good doctor Wei had called ahead and spoken to his associate Dr. Goldman who had been caring for my grandmother recently and was considered one of the better heart specialists in the city.

As luck would have it, Goldman had been making rounds at the hospital when my grandmother arrived and ordered her into ICU in an attempt to stabilize her heart. They had managed to bring her heart rate down from the wild palpitations of earlier. But the doctor had come out to speak with my mother and uncle and told them what all of us already knew.

Even though she was a tough woman she was older now and her body had been through a lot. He could not guarantee anything and told them both that her chances would be good if she made it through the night. There was nothing else to do but see if her will to live was stronger than the physical condition of her body. Even so we all knew that even if she did pull through on this one, we would all be here again very soon since her body was very weak and would eventually give out. This was the scene as explained to us by the doctor and everyone was aware of the odds in favor and against. No one really spoke other than to proceed with trying to contact the appropriate family members located out of town who had a need to know and to be here as support for my mother as best we could.

We all milled around making small talk about the simplest things while my mother and uncle and their first cousins and their in laws and all the others within their same age generation huddled together and discussed old family members already gone and how they had passed on. Some had horror stories of suffering while others thanked God for knowing that so and so had left in their sleep.

Strangely, they all exhibited this fear on their faces that if nothing else, they knew that at their ages, death was becoming more of an inevitability and for some, it was not that far off. They would huddle together and break off by themselves to ponder this alone by staring out the window or wandering aimlessly around the hallway.

I went over to my mother while she was deep in thought, kissed her forehead and held her hand trying to make it alright. My father was with her most of the time but the tension being experienced by us all led us to try and help give each other. We took turns comforting my mother. Each of us is trying to apply a fresh coat of strength to her will.

Finally the night dawned into a new day and we were told she would be moved up into a private room to be monitored more closely. This did not make sense to me and led me to believe they were probably trying to move her upstairs somewhere away from the ICU unit where others lay with still a fighting chance at life. My grandmother was not suffering from anything other than old age. The patients in ICU were younger, broken but fixable and facing a return to life as they had left it. My grandmother was dying.

While they prepped her to go upstairs, most of us went out for breakfast to the nearest restaurant with decent food. My mother and uncle remained behind to be there when they moved her. I promised to bring mom something back so she could eat. It was the first real meal some of us had since lunch the day before but no one was really hungry.

I brought my mother a small bowl of fruit and a burrito made of her *favorite chile verde con carne* even though I knew she would not touch the plate. "You have to eat something mama, you have to keep your strength up" I implored. She picked at some of the fruit and had one bite of the burrito but her stomach was so full of knots that she pushed the plate away. She only drank some of the Gatorade juice I had brought.

Then my mother called us together. All her children huddled into a small circle in the hallway outside the room upstairs. She told us that each of us would be allowed to go in and see her for no more than five minutes. This had been a wish of my grandmother and as usual, my mother was going to follow it to the letter. We were never really told but we all knew that it would be a quick five minutes to say goodbye.

All the years of life with this woman were filled with so many moments. You were to gather up emotional strength and in essence, suck it up and be strong and go on to say whatever you thought would be appropriate. A final goodbye wrapped into a five minute time period. What do you say in five minutes? The doctor who did not want to put her heart through more than what it could stand had placed the time limit. She was tired now and these would be her last few minutes on this earth.

I was chosen to go first because of my close connection to her, also since my sisters were too distraught to go in just yet. Not that I was in any better shape, but as directed, I sucked it up as I knew she would want me to. I slowly opened the door to her room with my stomach feeling the way it had that day. I told her I was leaving to join the military. This time though it was worse since there would be no return.

Gently, I opened the wide door leading into the room. My uncle was inside standing next to her holding her hand. She appeared half-asleep, struggling to keep her eyes open. She was groggy as if under the influence of the pain killing medication no doubt, codeine or methadone.

My uncle waved me into the room and nudged her gently to tell her I was there. He whispered into her ear and her eyes lit up at hearing him mention my name. Her eyes slowly moved to the foot of the bed as I came into her focus. The room was dim with little lighting and the rays of the bright sun outside were kept at bay by the tint on the window panes.

I held my breath and smiled for a minute, searching for something to say while trying to maintain composure that delayed the inevitable fate in store on this day. She smiled slowly, trying hard to focus on me as I came in and out of her line of sight in the drug induced euphoria she was experiencing.

"*Mi cabroncito*!" she said and with those words I thought I would lose it as I recalled all the times she used it as her special greeting for me.

"*Hola ama, ¿qué es esto que me dicen que estás mal? Nomas te estás mareando,*" I asked. "*Acaba con esta broma.*"

And she smiled again as she rubbed her eyes trying hard to remove the dizziness from her sight. "*No mijo, creo que esta vez es por seguro,*" she said in a soft tone. "*Ven aqui mi amor,*" she opened her arms and motioned me to her side.

My uncle released her and stepped back to allow me close to her. *"A ti, más que a todos voy a extrañar hijo mío,"* she sighed. "Remember all that I have told you and taught you for now. I will not be around to help guide you."

There was no more use in pretending. She knew the inevitable was coming, No more joking or smiling our way out of this one. I stared at her eyes both drowsy but stern in her look as a tear formed at the corner of my eye and dropped on the pillow to her side.

"Don't cry *mijo.* I only leave you in body but I will be in your soul forever. Always know that as long as you live I will be with you" she said and reached up to wipe another tear from my face.

"I'll miss you," were the only words I could form with my mouth.

She cupped my face in her hands and smiled. I could tell the drugs were keeping her in a state of semi-conscious she kept fighting to overcome

"I will miss you too *cabroncito*, but I will be here when you need me. Remember me and I will be there when you call. You are a part of me now and forever and nothing can ever take that away. Not even death," she said and motioned a soft wink at me as if to say I will defy even death to remain here, if you only believe, it will be so.

Her eyes reflected a sense of peace. At that point I came to understand what she had tried to make me believe that day long ago in the kitchen of her house. Being at peace with myself meant knowing that I was an extension of her. The lessons she provided me were instrumental in determining what type of person I would become. She had made the sacrifices and committed the mistakes. She had learned their invaluable lessons. Her desire for me had been to forewarn me of the perils and not have me commit the same mistakes and avoid the pain and the suffering. Her greatest wish was to pass on to her children and grandchildren the benefit of the lessons she had learned in life without having them make the same sacrifices. Not commit the mistakes but to learn to appreciate life as she had.

Yes, one does commit their own set of mistakes or bad decisions that one must learn from. If there is one great thing a parent wishes for a child, it is not to have them feel the pains and the hardships they went through. To not make the same mistakes for they knew the pain of the consequences. To learn to get up by themselves after one falls but to minimize the number of times they do by listening and learning from their own pitfalls. It is a lesson wrought from experience, initiated on by love, passed from one generation to the next and is the true essence of *aguante*.

I kissed her cheek and grabbed her hands in mine and slowly released them from the grip around my face. She smiled a last time and closed her eyes for a few seconds while her arms extended with mine. I stood next to her bed with her hands still locked in mine, refusing to let go of my palms. I stood up straight and took slow methodical steps back keeping her grip to my hand.

"Adios Ama," I said. "I love you."

She opened her eyes and smiled and said in her best English phrase, "I love you too *mi cabroncito, por siempre.*"

With that I released the grip from my hand and turned towards the door too choked up to think or say anything else. As I looked out the window there was not a cloud in the sky that day. It flashed its usual brightness of light in the midday sun but when I looked out the window again, the sky appeared in the darkest shade of gray that I had ever seen before in my life.

# CHAPTER SEVENTEEN

"And now ladies and gentlemen, the man you have all been waiting for. The man that I have worked with side by side for a good number of years and whom I find to be of a character second to none. He is a man like the rest of us and is thus not perfect, but you could not ask for a better definition of a true friend, confidant and leader. It has been my great pleasure to have worked with him but better yet to consider him my friend." Victor was looking at me from his place at the podium and I could tell his words were heartfelt.

In all the years I had known him, this was a serious side that I had never really seen. I was genuinely touched by his words of tribute.

"For all the times you were there because you had to be I say thanks, for all the times you were there because you wanted to be, words cannot express my appreciation" said Victor.

He was in a zone. The combination of reminiscence, admiration and the tequila were all working in conjunction and allowed him to speak so eloquently about our friendship.

"Have a good life my friend and remember there are those of us here who are better off for having known you and for sharing a little bit of life with you. C'mon up here dammit." he said as he opened his arms to embrace me where he stood.

The crowd stood to applaud and I felt a rush of euphoria come over me that was overwhelming. I stood up from my seat and walked over to give my partner and great friend a traditional Mexican *abrazo* from the heart.

We embraced like two men who had been through a lot together. But as is true in life, years full of living and sharing and creating good memories can come to a stop in the blink of an eye and when that time comes, you must embrace it for all it was. I had been determined not to choke up nor allow anyone else to do the same at this final farewell of mine. Now Victor was now making it extremely difficult.

I felt him relax his grip on me and pat my back a couple of times while I did the same. No words were said between two friends who had been through so many times, both good and bad, together.

While he turned and walked back to take his place with the others standing at the main table, I was faced with having to stare out at the crowd while attempting to gather my emotions enough to allow me to speak. The rush I experienced coupled with the glare from the bright lights focused on me prevented me from making out the faces in the crowd.

It took a while to focus on anyone and my eyes kept adjusting to the top of people's heads trying to make out faces or shapes under the many different hairstyles belonging to both men and women that were bobbing up and down. I myself kept bending slightly forward as I kept repeating myself to the many faces and blurs that whirled around me in a sea of applause.

"Thank you, thank you all," I said. It was a truly emotional moment I was experiencing and I tried hard at focusing on what I was about to say. I had prepared a small list of thank you's and farewells for some people. In the euphoria of the moment.

I decided it would be best to wing it and just remain with the emotions of the moment, wherever they may take me. I was still in the middle of trying to focus on the sea of people strategically placed around the dinner tables that stretched out all the way to the back of the gigantic banquet room. I was now able to pick out the faces in the near front and the groups around the tables in the middle area were also coming into focus.

Oh, how I wished everyone from the past could have lived long enough to be here and share this moment. The feeling of longing for their presence was starting to make that lump in my throat come up into my mouth and threatened to turn the smile on my face into a frown and act as a prelude to the tears that were welling up in my eyes. I tried hard to block out the memory of my parents, my grandparents and my aunts and uncles who had been so influential to me in my youth.

They were all gone now and for a moment I reflected on them as I looked down at the podium table pretending to adjust the microphone in front of me. In reality, I was doing this to keep from crying out in front of the audience gathered in front of me. Suddenly for a split second, as I finally started making out faces in the crowd and while waving my hands in a downward motion to have everyone stop applauding and take their chairs, I spotted a table in the back of the large room I was sure had not been there before. I stared at the group of people stationed around the large table as if in a dream. I stood mesmerized as I watched the table with the white tablecloth that seemed brighter in whiteness than the other tables and saw it sway to a gentle breeze which I found odd since there was no open window or open doorway. Other than the forced air coming down from the air conditioners up above, there was no breeze to speak of at all. Since the table was located in the back of the room close to the kitchen entrance, I thought perhaps it was the breeze caused by the kitchen doorway as it opened and closed to allow the waiters in and out of the area with their large trays now filled with the dessert entrees that were being passed out to all the tables. As my mind tried to grasp this possible scenario of the kitchen doorway being responsible for the swaying of the tablecloth, I shut my eyes hard and shook my head into focus, trying to gather my wits and refocus to make out the people at the table in the back. When I opened my eyes to shake the vision clear, I looked at the spot again and the table was gone. There was nothing there where I thought I had seen it before. Wait! I was sure there was a table there. I saw it! There were people standing around it, applauding, cheering and they were…it was my mother…and I… I saw my grandmother, but how…no, she…

Quickly, I gathered my wits and reminded myself that there was a large group of people here with me, staring at me, starting to sit down from the round of applause they had put up for me, and now they were sitting, pulling their chairs up to the table, anticipating, waiting, watching ready to hear me say something.

"I uhh, thank you everyone for that ovation, I ..uh," again I looked over at the spot where I had seen the table sway in the breeze with my grandmother, my mother, my father, my tia Josefina, my tia Aurora and all of them, standing there, proudly clapping for me, with smiles on their faces. But the table was not there anymore. It was there wasn't it? I saw it! Didn't I?

I held on to the sides of the podium to steady myself, "I appreciate all of you taking the time to come out here and spend some time with me on this my last day as a working man," I said to the crowd as I thought, the table had been there, hadn't it?

"I ...there are so many people that I wish to thank tonight." GET A GRIP ON YOURSELF, GET A GRIP! My fingers dug deep into the sides of the podium stand, so much so that my knuckles turned red from such a tight grip. "I want to of course, thank my wife who has stood by me all these years, putting up with the long hours and the times away from home" I said.

Ok, I thought, I think I'm coming back now. I looked back again at the back of the room and saw there was no table, nothing there.

“I want to thank Victor and all the guys for putting this event together. I want to say thanks for all the best wishes sent down from the main office in D.C., I appreciate you guys taking the time to come down for this,” I said.

I looked at Smith again who had that stupid grin on his and thought to myself no, on second thought, I really don’t.

“I wish to thank all my ex-bosses who I learned so much from, some of whom I see out there and who I appreciate for making the trip out here, good to see you guys again,” I said as I noticed Joe Thomas and Marcelo Santos from out west in the audience.

I was getting my comfort level back and I knew then that there had never been a table back there. It had just been but a figment of my imagination.

“Over the years, I attended many of these retirement dinners and the one thing I saw in common with them all was how the retiree, in this case me, marveled at how fast it all went by and how many people came into your life during that period. Well, I’m here to tell you all that it does go by fast and it’s hard to believe it until you actually stand up here and realize how many years it’s been since you began this voyage all those years ago,” I continued. “Earlier tonight, someone asked me who had been the most influential person in my career and in my life. I had not thought much about it until I realized how young I was when I first started and now after all these years, how many of those people who helped me when I first started are not here anymore. The people who molded me, who helped me become the man I am today. Those that stood by me and watched me grow and lent me their support so I could make it to today. To those of you here that helped me," I said as I looked at the audience. "I want to thank you for sharing some life with me, for allowing me to learn from you as you have learned from me. I acknowledge and am grateful for your presence here today but also, I wish to pay tribute to those who are not. Past friends and family who are no longer here."

I stared at the back of the room where I thought I had seen the table.

"I especially want to thank my mother and my grandmother who, though not here, remain with me in spirit today as they always have." I said in a solemn tone. I waved my hand in the air in a motion that covered all those in attendance down on the floor and said "I stand here humbled by the presence of you all here tonight. If there is but one wish I have, it would be to have those two women here tonight to share this special moment with me. Many of you honor me by placing me in the light of a person who is considerate, understanding and some say probably rightfully so, demanding. Though I apologize for my negatives, I believe my positives have always outweigh them. I am grateful for that. In fairness, I stand here as the humble product of the teachings instilled in me by those two special ladies. I am the result of their virtues and their wisdom, which molded me into the person I am today. If you come to pay tribute to what I was to each of you, then I in turn must pay tribute to them because I am a reflection of them and all those others who so influenced my life. I am blessed to be amongst such a large group of friends here today, but more than that I was blessed to have been raised by them both".

I stopped for a minute and in my thoughts I thanked god for having allowed me the opportunity to stand here at this moment. I had gone farther and achieved so much more than what even I had ever thought. Although I never discovered a cure for cancer or became someone rich and famous, my life had come to be far more than expected. I found a great peace within me. It had been a long way from the days of the old barrio, as a child running around barefoot playing in the street, as a teenager learning the wrong things from the wrong people, the addicts and the drunks, the fighters, the gamblers and the sinners. As an adult learning to understand that each of us is entrusted with a life, a life you can squander on nothing or change for the better by simply having faith in oneself and keeping the lessons of those who taught you right from wrong. Oh how I wished they had all lived to see this day, me standing here in front of all these people.

"I thank you for coming and I wish you all a good life" I said. The roar of approval to my words was evident by the applause that followed. I reached out and hugged a few of the people standing as I made my way back to my seat engulfed by the warm reception. A few more friends made it up the dais where more hugs were exchanged and photos were taken. Then, just like that, it was all over.

After the last few friends had made it out the door and tearful goodbyes exchanged with promises of staying in touch no matter what, I packed up my plaques and my awards and all the nice gifts that everyone had purchased and put them safely away in the car. The lights to the reception room were turned off and as we hugged Victor and his wife one last time with a promise to get together the following weekend.

We headed home. The moon shone bright in the night sky and there was a tinge of sentimentality alive in me as I reached for the CD holder that held all my Spanish music. I slipped the *"Mariachi Cobre toca las canciones de Jose Alfredo Jimenez"* disc into the CD player. It featured many of the old songs that reminded me of family get-togethers at my grandmother's house where everyone would sit outside listening to my brother David and Gordo and Kikirika play guitar while my grandmother sang the songs of heartbreak and of the drinking that accompanied the heartbreak. On the drive home with the chords of the first melody filling the car with music, I recalled all the memories I had relieved that evening and my mind once again drifted back to my people.

My tia Aurora passed away in Los Angeles a little bit after my grandmother died. She had been struggling with cancer for about a year during the time my grandmother had been very sick and had been so bad off she had not been able to come out and see her mother before she passed away. The last time mother and daughter were together had been a couple of years before my grandmother passed and at the time, neither had any idea it would be the last time they would get to see each other. My tia had been planning a trip to see her mother before she took ill but the doctors in LA had advised her not to travel due to the strain. So she would call my mother and get daily reports on her mother's condition while relaying reports on her own medical progress.

It had been extremely hard on my LA cousins to let go of their mother. Even with all the toughness they exhibited and all the street bravado they were known for, the heartache still showed on their faces. It reflected a side of them I had not seen before but one that reinforced my belief about them. They were not gangland killers playing some role in a movie about East L.A. Chicano toughs, as they liked to show. They were after all human beings with good hearts and they were dealing with the same emotions that overcome us all. They lived in a world dictated by street perceptions but yet they hurt inside just like the rest of us and it was showing on them and it was OK.

We were familia and we all grieved and we all got through it together. My tia had been a good hearted woman who loved to laugh. Her character possessed the same rough qualities of her mother and of my tia Josefina but she was more like my mother, exhibiting a more calm and reserved manner. She looked up to her older sister Anita and in turn, my mother adored her little sister. After my grandmother's death when we found out she had passed, I again went out to California with my parents and helped my mother bury yet another sister. My cousins reeling from the loss of the glue to their family pretty much fell apart. At the funeral, my cousin Lori chided me on how I needed to appreciate the fact that my mother was still here with me to enjoy. I replied by saying I had realized this fact many years before.

# CHAPTER EIGHTEEN

My mother's death had been a far more agonizing experience than I thought it would be. In the time after my grandmother's death, I felt my mother had somehow lost an immeasurable part of her desire for life. Whether she was conscious of it or not and also considering the extreme closeness to her mother, it was evident that the loss had become more and more of an extreme pain to bear. At the time, I thought to myself that she was searching for an answer in her quest to fill the void left by the departure of her close partner. Marriage to my father had appeared fulfilling and having her children and grandchildren around had been a great help in dealing with the pain. Yet nothing could overcome the feeling of loss she struggled with every day. I tried to get her to talk about it in the belief that expressing her pain in words would help lessen her burden. After all, I was her son. Someone she could confide in, someone who understood her and the special bond that had existed between the two for so many years. Someone who had been at the center of a tug of war between the two women and who was grieving just the same in having lost someone so special.

"Mamá, siéntate y vamos a jugar baraja" I would say. She had always liked playing cards and surely she would welcome a game with me just to sit and talk and pass the time away. But no, not even this would get her going again.

"No hijo, no tengo ganas" she would reply and go back to what she was doing, preparing dinner for my father or knitting something in her chair or just sitting and staring out the window lost in her thoughts. I truly felt for her but no matter what I nor anyone else for that matter was able to reach her where she most needed someone to be. This I would later figure was the root of the problem.

The one spot she yearned for someone to be at could not be filled by any of us. The void was too great and the shadow loomed too large over us and could only be filled by one person. On top of the mourning over her loss was the added burden of the medical condition she was now facing. About a year before my grandmother passed, she was diagnosed with cancer. This came at a time when my mother was focused on caring for her mother in her last few months of life and was coupled with the burden of worrying about her little sister in California who suffered from the same condition. Then as now, the fact that cancer runs through this family is a fact that never leaves me.

The doctors had diagnosed it in my mother early on that year and initial treatments of chemotherapy and radiation had at first been successful. But after a period of time and just before my grandmother's death it came back with a vengeance. This new diagnosis led to a struggle with whether to return to the regular treatments of radiation into her body that forced her to deal with the nausea, the hair loss and the weight loss or as it appeared she was leaning towards, to just forget about it. Ready to let the dreaded disease have its way.

At the time of the first diagnosis by the doctors, my grandmother was still alive. We all knew this was the spark that kept her going. I remember her desire to battle the disease with everything she had. But after my grandmother was gone, I felt my mother had lost her desire and her strength. She had given up all hope and she wanted to fight no more. This reasoning, more than anything else, was the biggest factor in her decision not to continue in the futile effort to overcome the disease.

This pained me so of course since I wanted her to continue to fight and remain here on this earth with us. She was tired. The doctors told us all that a critical factor in the element of recovery is a strong will to live. In this case, I noticed that her will to fight was no longer there. The loss of her mother, the fatigue and the many years of battling had all worn her down. The prospect of continuing treatments and doctor visits and hospital visits and all that was necessary to maintain the fight was just prolonging what she felt was inevitable. She felt she had no more to give. During it all, I knew she had but one wish and that was to remain on this earth long enough to care for her mother. To cheat death by stalling and allow her mother to go first so that she would be there to care for her till the end. This desire was made evident to me at the time we first spoke about the cancer when she was initially diagnosed.

"I only pray for one thing *mijo*, and that is God keeps me alive long enough to let me care for my mother until her last day," she said to me in the living room of the house on Yandell Street where I had grown up.

I was devastated when I received her call to tell me of the diagnosis and

I had immediately gone to see her at the house. We sat down and in her usual aura of defiance and self-confidence, she tried to reassure me that the diagnosis was just another of life's obstacles she would no doubt overcome.

"You must promise me one thing," she had said and looked me straight in the eyes but before she even said it, I knew what the request would be. "You must never mention this cancer to your abuela, you must never let her know. This is a secret I will keep between my children, my husband and myself. My mother does not need to worry about this," she said.

At the time, I knew she was asking this to keep her mother from worrying about her condition while, as it seemed to me, having no regard for her own well being. The latter part of this request being the only issue that troubled me. What if something happens and she takes a turn for the worst, I thought? What would we do if the disease accelerates and takes her faster than what the doctors expect? What if…

"Mama, I don't think…" I started to say.

"YES AND I DON'T WANT YOU TO THINK, I just want you to do as I ask!" she replied in a stern voice. She made it clear she was not asking for my opinion on this. "Please *hijo mio*, do it for me" she pleaded with me and her soft brown eyes reached into my very soul as she cupped my hand in hers.

As any good Mejicano son would do when asked by his mother to do something he would not consider doing for anyone else, I had no choice but to honor her wishes.

"OK mama, I promise, don't worry, I won't say anything to my grammar," I said.

Now all these years later as I'm driving home on this special night set aside for me and I listen to the CD player below the sweet serenade of the mariachi violins creeping into my very being. The *tololoche* kept the deep bass rhythm pounding into my soul, hearing the balladeer's voice sing the words of pain and the trumpets gently wailing the soft melody of the song in the background, I remembered how that moment more than anything else defined the lesson learned of my mother.

More than anything else, from her I learned the lessons of compassion and caring in their most extreme form. Truth be told, my mother could be a cold, hard woman when she wanted to be. The result of living a life as a mother at age sixteen and the responsibilities that come with it along with the shared burden of helping raise her siblings had taught her to develop a hard, tough skin. My mother was not the easiest person to get along with as at times can be evident in my own demeanor. The fact of the matter is that when my mother cared for someone, especially someone as close as family, she would give up the last piece of food she had to help that person even if it meant she would starve. She was a person of compassionate heart buried under strong bricks of fortitude who refused to accept defeat in the everyday struggle with life. Her own strength was inherited from her mother but her compassion was learned from living a life conquered by its unfairness and understanding its effect on the vanquished.

In the end, she decided against treatments and agreed only to remain on painkillers to get her through the pain from the sickness ravaging her body. This way she felt she remained sharp enough and strong enough to continue to attend to the needs of her mother in her last few days. She refused to compromise even with death and was determined to fulfill this dedication to the end and by God she did. As the news of the second diagnosis of cancer came around, I think she felt she could fight no more forever. The way she saw it, she had lived enough for two lifetimes and figured that if it was time to go, then so be it. The one bit of happiness she savored was she felt God had granted her the wish of having outlived her mother. Now she would not worry about entrusting someone else to care for her mother as she felt there was no one else worthy. It was an amazing thing for me to see. That one person would want something so badly as to give of oneself for another. This is the lesson I remember and that will always remain with me about my mother.

It was then that the time had finally come when she was no longer able to care for herself at home and the hospital visits became more and more frequent as the doctors told us there was nothing more they could do. They gave us a choice of leaving her there at the hospital or of taking her home to the family surroundings that she would be more familiar with. My oldest sister Irene had agreed to bring her home one last time and I was very proud of her for that. I thought this a fitting tribute by my sister as the eldest continued to do for my mother what ours had done for hers. In my last conversation with her before she succumbed to death I found myself conversing with my mother in the traditional family way of making believe that tomorrow everything would be OK, that everything was going to be fine. This was a trait I had learned from both mother and daughter and was the only way I knew to face something so difficult.

"*Andale* mama, tomorrow is your last day here in the hospital and you gotta get better so we can go home and play cards" I said.

It was tough to walk in and play the game of pretend with my mother and my teacher. I tried so hard to exemplify the lessons I had learned by imitating them both in being strong in this way and now, sparring with her here when her physical condition made it tough on both of us and impossible for her to be anything but miserable was nothing short of unbearable.

"Come on now, you promised me you were going to make some homemade *tortillas* tomorrow and you can't back out now. I'll go buy some of that New Mexico *chile* you like so much and we can roast it and mix it up with *tomate y ajo* and just eat burritos de *chile* like we used to, *te acuerdas mamá*?" I would say to her.

She would not respond to me but just lay in bed, shriveled up in pain, skinny from the lack of food, painkillers running through her veins and forcing a half smile as she understood what I was trying to do. She wanted to show me she appreciated my efforts at trying to bring her back to a mood she could now only recall as a memory.

"*Tas loco chistoso,*" she would say and smile meekly.

The end was near and she had lost the will to live. Even if her mind wanted to, her body was just not responding to the orders it was given so we just sat and watched the old Mexican movies on the Spanish stations that featured Cantinflas and Maria Felix, Viruta y Chapulin and even the ones with La India Maria that she liked so much. I would sit in a chair next to her and hold her hand while she lay in bed and we watched TV together. I would keep one eye on the tube while checking her condition with the other. The doctors had said it would be a matter of time but said they could not be more specific. After a while, I really came to hate those damn doctors. I took comfort in seeing her eyes light up at the antics of La India Maria on the TV even if it was just a temporary joy. Later I would steal another glance and notice her eyes tightly closed fighting off the pain even in the drug induced sleep.

The memory I will always have of my mother is that of a strong woman dedicated to caring for those she loved, defeated in her old age only by the advances of a pathetically incurable disease. My sister fixed up a nice room for her with a hospital bed that she got from the hospice people. She brought all the little ceramic clowns from the collection that my mother kept in a display cabinet at the house on Yandell Street. They were all in different poses made of vibrant colors that reflected the sadness and the joy of life by the smiles and the frowns on their faces. Anytime any of us went someplace out of town or out of the country or on the few times she and my father had gone to Las Vegas on their gambling getaways, each of us would always try and bring back a unique clown to add to her collection. They made her happy and she took care of her collection and always told visitors to the house that this one was from here and that one was from there. It was her one private joy in life, collecting little clown figurines to make her smile.

My sister placed them all around the room so she could see them surround her, bringing a smile to her face and to remind her of the past. She liked looking at them before she drifted off to sleep. She died on a Sunday morning in October, when gray fall days started to give way to the cold short days of a pending winter in the desert.

# CHAPTER NINETEEN

The house lights came on as I eased the car up the driveway by way of the automatic lighting system that kicked in with the touch of a button on top of the car dashboard. The house seemed a lot bigger now since my daughter had married and moved away. She lived with my two grandchildren on the other side of town and the big house seemed larger than what was needed for two people. It was just the two of us now and although my wife had come from a big family and we had bought a big house with the intention of sharing in family get-togethers and enjoying BBQ's to relive the good times we had growing up in large families, it had not come to be. Family infighting and jealousies and stubbornness had prevented anything of the sort from coming true. It seemed someone was always mad at someone else or so and so won't be here if so and so comes and on and on it went. No more did we enjoy the experience of having family come together with children running around and men talking sports while *carne asada* was cooking on the grill. There were no more *pachangas* with *cabrito* cooking in a fire pit that filled the air with the strong aroma of tenderized meat. No more gatherings of women and wives in the kitchen having mixed drinks and laughing about their husbands and boyfriends while mixing and cutting up gobs of *chile verde* and onions and cilantro.

Things had changed and the special times from family bonding where the older generations passed on the wisdom of their ways to the younger ones was no longer evident in our lives. We had both been mistaken in our belief that traditional family customs would live on forever and that our brothers and sisters felt the same. The lack of cohesiveness in the family was not my fault, it was not the fault of my brothers and sisters, it was not the fault of my cousins. It was the fault of us all. Not to say that everyone in the families wasn't getting along but life was different now and each family member followed the beat of their own drummer. Even all my California cousins drifted off into their own worlds and contact with them was now few and far in between compared to the way things used to be. As the saying goes, things change I guess and besides, I had friends whose families still got together in the tradition of the old ways and even they confided in me that there seemed to be more hassles now when everyone got together and it wasn't necessarily like the old days for them either.

I'm sure that some families still keep some of the traditional family get-together values alive. In ours, things had changed to the point where for example on Christmas day, other than the joy experienced with my grandchildren and sharing the look of excitement on their faces, the holidays were just not what they used to be anymore. This had been the purpose of buying a big house to keep the old traditions going. Done with a hope that memories of the past could be kept alive by those entrusted with them. But it did not come to be and now the big house only seemed like an empty shell of a tribute to a long ago wish.

I parked the car in the garage space and figured I would leave all the gifts and the mementos of twenty-five years of a working life in place until the next day. I was emotionally spent and not in the mood to carry bags and boxes into the house late at night. I went inside and poured myself a drink of Tequila Sauza into a glass with a lemon on the side and grabbed the saltshaker from the kitchen to go upstairs.

The master bedroom had two large glass doors that opened up to a balcony on the side that overlooked the neighborhood and provided an extravagant view of the city skyline. I liked to sit outside on the porch sometimes and allow my thoughts to flow free after a hard day at work or just to enjoy the view. I opened the sliding door and placed the bottle and the glass on a small table set outside as I pulled up a chair to sit and gaze out at the night sky. It was a clear cool night filled with stars that reached all the way across the sky and seemed to end at the jagged tops of the Franklin mountain range off in the distance. The air was still without even so much as a breeze and the quiet and solitude of the late night enveloped me like a blanket that surrounded me on all sides. The light chill in the air quickly vanished from my body with the help of the strong alcoholic content in the tequila and the lemon and the salt served to chase away the sting that lingered in my throat. It was over now and it was just me and my thoughts to keep me company.

Looking back and having gone through it all now, I felt I had been really blessed. I was still in good health and had managed to keep the company of a good woman by my side. There were still many things in my life that I wished to accomplish and I was still relatively young and though I was not swimming in money, I was now financially well off enough to make them happen. The journey from the small house in the barrio to this two-story home had been one of devotion and sacrifice but up to now had been well worth it. I poured another bit of tequila into the shot glass and admitted to myself that I would not have been here if not for the grace of God and because of all those people in my life. I closed my eyes and while hoping that God wasn't too busy somewhere else listening to someone who was truly in need at this particular time. I thought it was appropriate to say a little prayer of thanks. "Dear Lord," I began, "Thank you for everything you have granted me and all in my life which has come to pass that allows me to be here today. Thank you for having kept me safe and for giving me the strength to have everything come out OK. I sit here humbled by your guidance and blessed by your protection," I said.

I opened my eyes for a minute and thought about my people one last time. "And Lord, I know that grandma Lencha is up there with you and probably giving you a hard time by asking for a whiskey and coke or yelling for one of her cigarettes but please be kind to her. She's a good lady and next time you see her, tell her I miss her. Tell my mother I'm OK and that we all miss her down here too. And tell everyone else up there, my father, my tia's, and granpa Joe that I did OK, that I hope they're proud of me because

I would not have been able to do it without them, all of them." I said. I opened my eyes and quickly felt a strange sense of euphoria enter my body. I couldn't really tell whether it was the tequila or the emotion of the moment that I was experiencing so I paused for a moment. Although it was a sensation that began in my stomach, it seemed to peak inside me with a sense of satisfaction that I found to be very comforting. After a minute had passed a smile of satisfaction began to spread across my face.

I knew immediately what the feeling of sensation was that was inside of me. It was my inner peace. The peace wished upon me by my grandmother and my mother. It engulfed me in a comfort such as that from a warm embrace and relaxed me in what seemed like a state of content. I had achieved what had been most important to those who had loved me. And as I sat in its warm glow and enjoyed the spiritual comfort it afforded me, I thought for a moment that perhaps I was wrong. Maybe it was just the tequila that was starting to take control of my six senses. Maybe it was just the liquor talking and not my real peace. As a twinge of disappointment came over me from realizing that this could be the only true rational explanation for it, deep inside I asked God for some type of sign. Something that would negate my rational thinking and make me believe that what I experienced was truly a connection to the comfort bestowed upon me.

In the backyard of my house, there are two maple trees that stand tall and firm from years of growth where they were planted there many years ago. My two grandchildren still loved to come over and play in the thick leafy branches that spread out over the vast yard and which provide cool relief from the hot summer days in the desert. Many times, I myself had sat in the large shade at the bottom provided by the old trees and had even fallen asleep during afternoons spent outside playing with the girls. But on this night, we still had no breeze to speak of, I sat in the chair on the balcony embarrassed at myself by the foolish request I had asked of the good Lord. When just then the leaves on the trees began to sway from a strong breeze. The leafy tops of the two trees moved in unison with each other as the cool breeze penetrated its branches and caused some leaves to fall to the ground and race across the yard in an array of fascinating motion. I looked at the trees swaying and I looked out at the yards across the neighborhood. There was no breeze moving any other trees in the yards around me. I looked back at my trees and after a minute they came to an abrupt stop.

I smiled. If this was not a true sign then I did not know what else is. I looked up at the night sky towards the heavens and they appeared as peaceful of a scene as I had never seen before. "Thank you," I said as the inner sensation of peace came back to me to rest within my soul as it found its permanent place.

I picked up the shot glass full of tequila and decided I needed nothing else to alter my feeling at the moment. I emptied the glass over the railing of the balcony and placed the glass back on the table. As I stood up from my chair I gazed over to the maple trees one last time and they appeared in the night light as they had always been, strong, firm and comforting in their pose. I walked over and opened the glass door into the bedroom now dark and quiet and slid the door closed behind me.

I went to my side of the bed and undressed with nothing but the light of the moon up above shining through the sliding glass doors. I was about to place my wallet on the night stand beside me and noticed there was something there on top next to the lamp. Quietly, I turned on the low level light and saw that it was one of the small porcelain clown figurines that my sister had given me after my mother died. She told me that my mother had told her to make sure she gave it to me because she had wanted me to have it. It had its place on the dresser facing the nightstand and I had no idea what it was doing there. But then I thought about it and I knew.

It was a small caricature figurine made of porcelain and no bigger than six inches. It was of Emmit the clown with his trademark torn coat in black and his bolo hat tilted to the side. He had a frown on his face with the fuzzy beard and he was carrying his famous stick with a handkerchief tied at the end slung over his shoulder. It had been one of my mother's favorites and one of the first ones she had bought at some doll show a long, long time ago. I smiled as I remembered how I had once mentioned to her how much I had liked it with its intricate detail and how the clown reflected such sadness in his eyes. I placed it back on the nightstand by the bed. I smiled at it and left it there on its place by the mantle as I turned off the lights and went to sleep.

THIS BOOK IS DEDICATED TO THE FOLLOWING PEOPLE.

To my wife Letty for always believing in me. To my friend Norma for always having pushed me. To my father and to my mother and of course to my grandma Lencha without whom this book would never have been possible. I hope I did you proud.

www.ingramcontent.com/pod-product-compliance
Lightning Source LLC
Chambersburg PA
CBHW010552170726
48285CB00011B/2878

* 9 7 8 1 9 5 3 4 4 7 1 8 0 *